THE DUST OFF THEIR FEET

lessons from the first church

THE BOOK OF ACTS RETOLD BY BRIAN MCLAREN

COMMENTARY ESSAYS BY:

Chris Se

ARTICLES BY:

David Capes	Tim Keel
Robert Creech	Evan Lauer
Greg Garrett	Kerry Shook
Andrew Jones	Chuck Smith, Jr.

the voice

A SCRIPTURE PROJECT TO REDISCOVER THE STORY OF THE BIBLE

NELSON BIBLES
A Division of Thomas Nelson Publishers
Since 1798

www.thomasnelson.com

The Dust Off Their Feet: Lessons from the First Church
Copyright © 2006 Thomas Nelson, Inc.

the voice.
Copyright © 2006 Ecclesia Bible Society
Published by Thomas Nelson, Inc.
Nashville, TN 37214
www.thomasnelson.com
Published in association with Eames Literary Services, Nashville, TN
Typesetting by Brecca Theele
Cover Design by Scott Lee Designs / www.scottleedesigns.com

Printed in the United States of America
1 2 3 4 5 6 7 8 9—14 13 12 11 10 09 08 07 06

Contributors

The Dust Off Their Feet: Lessons from the First Church

Scriptures retold by: Brian McLaren

Commentary Essays written by: Chris Seay

Contribution to articles by:
David Capes
Robert Creech
Greg Garrett
Andrew Jones
Tim Keel
Evan Lauer
Chris Seay
Kerry Shook
Chuck Smith, Jr.

Scholarly review by:
David Capes
Darrell L. Bock

Editorial review by:
Maleah Bell
James F. Couch, Jr.
Marilyn Duncan
Amanda Haley
Kelly Hall
Merrie Noland

A SCRIPTURE PROJECT TO REDISCOVER THE STORY OF THE BIBLE

TABLE OF CONTENTS

Section Two // **The Evolving Church in Acts**

Section Three // **The Evolving Church of Today**

Section Four // **An Excerpt from *The Last Eyewitness***

Any literary project reflects the age in which it is written. **The Voice** is created for and by a church in great transition. Throughout the body of Christ, extensive discussions are ongoing about a variety of issues including style of worship, how we separate culture from our theology, and what is essential truth. In fact, we are struggling with what is truth. At the center of this discussion is the role of Scripture. This discussion is heating up with strong words being exchanged. Instead of furthering the division over culture and theology, it is time to bring the body of Christ together again around the Bible. Thomas Nelson Publishers and Ecclesia Bible Society together are developing Scripture products that foster spiritual growth and theological exploration out of a heart for worship and mission. We have dedicated ourselves to hearing and proclaiming God's voice through this project.

Previously most Bibles and biblical reference works were produced by professional scholars writing in academic settings. **The Voice** uniquely represents collaboration among scholars, pastors, writers, musicians, poets, and other artists. The goal is to create the finest Bible products to help believers experience the joy and wonder of God's revelation. Four key words describe the vision of this project:

- holistic // considers heart, soul, and mind
- beautiful // achieves literary and artistic excellence
- sensitive // respects cultural shifts and the need for accuracy
- balanced // includes theologically diverse writers and scholars

Uniqueness of *The Voice*

About 40 different human authors are believed to have been inspired by God to write the Scriptures. **The Voice** retains the perspective of the human writers. Most English translations attempt to even out the styles of the different authors in sentence structure and vocabulary. Instead, **The Voice** distinguishes sentence structure and vocabulary of each author. The heart of the project is retelling the story of the Bible in a form that is as fluid as modern literary works yet that remains true to the original manuscripts. First, accomplished writers create an English rendering; then, respected Bible scholars adjust the rendering to align the manuscript with the original texts. Attention is paid to the use of idioms, artistic elements, confusion of pronouns, repetition of conjunctives, modern sentence structure, and the public reading of the passage. In the process, the writer or scholar may adjust the arrangement of words or expand the phrasing to create an English equivalent.

To help the reader understand how the new rendering of a passage compares to the original manuscripts, several indicators are imbedded within the text. Italic type indicates words not directly tied to a dynamic translation of the original language. Material delineated by a screened box or set apart in a box expands on the theme. This portion is not taken directly from the original language. To avoid the endless repetition of simple conjunctives, dialog is formatted as a screenplay. The speaker is indicated, the dialog is indented, and quotation marks are not used. This helps greatly in the public reading of Scripture. Sometimes the original text includes exposition that interrupts the dialog. This is shown either as a stage direction immediately following the speaker's name or as part of the narrative section that immediately precedes the speaker's name. The screenplay format clearly shows who is speaking.

Throughout *The Voice,* other language devices improve readability. We follow the standard conventions used in most translations regarding textual evidence. *The Voice* is based on the earliest and best manuscripts from the original languages (Greek, Hebrew, and Aramaic). When significant variations influence a reading, we follow the publishing standard by bracketing the passage and placing a note in the margin or at the bottom of the page while maintaining the traditional chapter and verse divisions. The footnotes reference quoted material and help the reader understand the translation for a particular word. Words that are borrowed from another language or words that are not common outside of the theological community (such as baptism, repentance, and salvation) are translated into more common terminology. For clarity, some pronouns are replaced with their antecedents. Word order and parts of speech are sometimes altered to help the reader understand the original passage.

— Ecclesia Bible Society

About *The Voice* Project

As retold, edited, and illustrated by a gifted team
of writers, scholars, poets, and storytellers

A New Way to Process Ideas

Chris Seay's vision for *The Voice* goes back 15 years to his early attempts to teach the Bible in the narrative as the story of God. As western culture has moved into what is now referred to as postmodernism, Chris observed that the way a new generation processes ideas and information raises obstacles to traditional methods of teaching biblical content. His desire has grown to open the Bible in ways that overcome these obstacles to people coming to faith. Instead of propositional-based thought patterns, people today are more likely to interact with events and individuals through complex observations involving emotions, thought processes, tactile experiences, and spiritual awareness. Much as in the parables of Jesus and in the metaphors of the prophets, narrative communication touches the whole person.

Hence, out of that early vision comes the need in a postmodern culture to present Scripture in a narrative form. The result is a retelling of the Scriptures: *The Voice*, not of words, but of meaning and experience.

The Timeless Narrative

The Voice is a fresh expression of the timeless narrative known as the Bible. Stories that were told to emerging generations of God's goodness by their grandparents and tribal leaders were recorded and assembled to form the Christian Scriptures. Too often, the passion, grit, humor, and beauty has been lost in the translation process. *The Voice* seeks to recapture what was lost.

From these early explorations by Chris and others has come *The Voice*: a Scripture project to rediscover the story of the Bible. Thomas Nelson Publishers and Ecclesia Bible Society have joined together to stimulate unique creative experiences and to develop Scripture products and resources to foster spiritual growth and theological exploration out of a heart for the mission of the church and worship of God.

Traditional Translations

Putting the Bible into the language of modern readers has too often been a painstaking process of correlating the biblical languages to the English vernacular. The Bible is filled with passages intended to inspire, captivate, and depict beauty. The old school of translation most often fails at attempts to communicate beauty, poetry, and story. *The Voice* is a collage of compelling narratives, poetry, song, truth, and wisdom. *The Voice* will call you to enter into the whole story of God with your heart, soul, and mind.

A New Retelling

One way to describe this approach is to say that it is a "soul translation," not just a "mind translation." But "translation" is not the right word. It is really the retelling of the story. The "retelling" involves translation and paraphrase, but mostly entering into the story of the Scriptures and recreating the event for our culture and time. It doesn't ignore the role of scholars, but it also values the role of writers, poets, songwriters, and artists. Instead, teams of scholars partner with a writer to blend the mood and voice of the original author with an accurate rendering of words of the text in English.

The Voice is unique in that it represents collaboration among scholars, writers, musicians, and other artists. Its goal is to create the finest Bible products to help believers experience the joy and wonder of God's revelation. In this time of great transition within the church, we are seeking to give gifted individuals opportunities to craft a variety of products and experiences: a translation of the Scriptures, worship music, a worship film festival, biblical art, worship conferences, gatherings of creative thinkers, a Web site for individuals and churches to share biblical resources, and books derived from exploration during the Bible translation work.

The heart of each product within *The Voice* project is the retelling of the Bible story. To accomplish the objectives of the project and to facilitate the various products envisioned within the project, the Bible text is being translated. We trust that this retelling will be a helpful contribution to a fresh engagement with Scripture. The Bible is the greatest story ever told, but it often doesn't read like it. *The Voice* brings the biblical narratives to life and reads more like a great novel than the traditional versions of the Bible that are seldom opened in contemporary culture.

Readable and Enjoyable

A careful process is being followed to assure that the spiritual, emotional, and artistic goals of the project are met. First, the retelling of the Bible has been designed to be readable and enjoyable by emphasizing the narrative nature of Scripture. Beyond simply providing a set of accurately translated individual words, phrases, and sentences, our teams were charged to render the biblical texts with sensitivity to the flow of the unfolding story. We asked them to see themselves not only as guardians of the sacred text, but also as storytellers, because we believe that the Bible has always been intended to be heard as the sacred story of the people of God. We assigned each literary unit (for example, the writings of John or Paul) to a team that included a skilled writer and biblical and theological scholars, seeking to achieve a mixture of scholarly expertise and literary skill.

Personal and Diverse

Second, as a consequence of this team approach, *The Voice* is both personal and diverse. God used about 40 human instruments to communicate His message, and each one has a unique voice or literary style. Standard translations tend to flatten these individual styles so that each book reads more or less like the others—with a kind of impersonal textbook-style prose. Some translations and paraphrases have paid more attention to literary style—but again, the literary style of one writer, no matter how gifted, can unintentionally obscure the diversity of the original voices. To address these problems, we asked our teams to try to feel and convey the diverse literary styles of the original authors.

Faithful

Third, we have taken care that *The Voice* is faithful and that it avoids prejudice. Anyone who has worked with translation and paraphrase knows that there is no such thing as a completely unbiased or objective translation. So, while we do not pretend to be purely objective, we asked our teams to seek to be as faithful as possible to the biblical message as they understood it together. In addition, as we partnered biblical scholars and theologians with our writers, we intentionally built teams that did not share any single theological tradition. Their diversity has helped each of them not to be trapped within his or her own individual preconceptions, resulting in a faithful and fresh rendering of the Bible.

Stimulating and Creative

Fourth, we have worked hard to make *The Voice* both stimulating and creative. As we engaged the biblical text, we realized again and again that certain terms have conventional associations for modern readers that would not have been present for the original readers—and that the original readers would have been struck by certain things that remain invisible or opaque to modern readers. Even more, we realized that modern readers from different religious or cultural traditions would hear the same words differently. For example, when Roman Catholic or Eastern Orthodox readers encounter the word "baptism," a very different set of meanings and associations come to mind than those that would arise in the minds of Baptist or Pentecostal readers. And a secular person encountering the text would have still different associations. The situation is made even more complex when we realize that *none* of these associations may resemble the ones that would have come to mind when John invited Jewish peasants and Pharisees into the water of the Jordan River in the months before Jesus began His public ministry. It is far harder than most people realize to help today's readers recapture the original impact of a single word like "baptism." In light of this challenge, we decided, whenever possible, to select words that would stimulate fresh thinking rather than reinforce unexamined assumptions. We want the next generation of Bible readers—whatever their background—to have the best opportunity possible to hear God's message the way the first generation of Bible readers heard it.

Transformative

Finally, we desire that this translation will be useful and transformative. It is all too common in many of our Protestant churches to have only a few verses of biblical text read in a service, and then that selection too often becomes a jumping-off point for a sermon that is at best peripherally related to, much less rooted in, the Bible itself. The goal of *The Voice* is to promote the public reading of longer sections of Scripture—followed by thoughtful engagement with the biblical narrative in its richness and fullness and dramatic flow. We believe the Bible itself, in all its diversity and energy and dynamism, is the message; it is not merely the jumping-off point.

The various creations of the project bring creative application of commentary and interpretive tools. These are clearly indicated and separated from the Bible text that is drawn directly from traditional sources. Along with the creative resources and fresh expressions of God's Word, the reader has the benefit of centuries of biblical research applied dynamically to our rapidly changing culture.

The products underway in *The Voice* include dynamic and interactive presentations of the critical passages in the life of Jesus and the early church, recorded musical presentation of Scripture originally used in worship or uniquely structured for worship, artwork commissioned from young artists, dramatized audio presentations from the Gospels and the Old Testament historical books, film commentary on our society using the words of Scripture, and exploration of the voice of each human author of the Bible.

The first product for *The Voice*, entitled *The Last Eyewitness: The Final Week*, released Spring 2006, follows Jesus through His final week of life on earth through the firsthand account of John the apostle. This book combines the drama of the text with the artwork of Rob Pepper into a captivating retelling of Jesus' final days.

Forthcoming projects include *The Voice of Matthew*, a retelling of the Gospel by Lauren Winner (author of *Girl Meets God* and *Real Sex*); *Eyewitness Live*, an audio dramatization of the Gospel of John; and *The Voice of Luke*, in which Luke sets the record straight with a doctor's analytical mind.

The Team

The team writing *The Voice* brings unprecedented gifts to this unique project. An award-winning fiction writer, an acclaimed poet, a pastor renowned for using art and narrative in his preaching and teaching, Greek and Hebrew authorities, and biblical scholars are all coming together to capture the beauty and diversity of God's Word.

Writers

The writers for *The Voice* who have contributed to *The Dust Off Their Feet: Lessons from the First Church* are:

> **Bible Text: Brian McLaren**—internationally known speaker and author of ten
> books, including *A New Kind of Christian* and *A Generous Orthodoxy*.
> **Commentary Essays: Chris Seay**—church planter, pastor, president of Ecclesia Bible
> Society, and internationally acclaimed speaker. His previous books include *The
> Gospel Reloaded* (coauthored with Greg Garrett), *The Gospel According to Tony
> Soprano*, and *Faith of My Fathers* (with his father and grandfather).

Other writers for *The Voice* who contributed to the articles in *The Dust Off Their Feet* are:

David Capes—Chair of the Department of Christianity and Philosophy at Houston Baptist University.

Robert Creech—senior pastor of University Baptist Church of Houston, Texas, and author of articles in numerous journals and reference works.

Greg Garrett—professor of film and writing at Baylor University and author of several books, including *Free Bird* and *Cycling*.

Andrew Jones— pastor and international consultant for the Baptist General Convention of Texas and DAWN Ministries.

Tim Keel—pastor of Jacob's Well in Kansas City, Missouri.

Evan Lauer—pastor of Coastlands Church of Pacific Beach, California, and a writer for *Planet* magazine.

Kerry Shook—senior pastor of Fellowship of The Woodlands of Houston, Texas.

Chuck Smith, Jr.—senior pastor of Capo Beach Calvary, Capistrano Beach, California, and author of three books, including *There Is A Season: Authentic, Innovative Ministry in Popular Culture*.

The two critical reviewers of *The Dust Off Their Feet* are:

David Capes, PhD—Chair of the Department of Christianity and Philosophy at Houston Baptist University. He has written several books, including *The Footsteps of Jesus in the Holy Land*.

Darrell L. Bock, PhD—Research Professor of New Testament Studies at Dallas Theological Seminary, Elder Emeritus at Trinity Fellowship Church, Contributing Editor at *Christianity Today*, and author of commentaries on Mark, Luke, and Acts, as well as of a book on Jesus and Scripture.

Other writers for *The Voice,* who are working on forthcoming products, include:

Eric Bryant, pastor/author

Tara Leigh Cobble, singer/songwriter

Don Chaffer, singer/songwriter, poet
Lori Chaffer, singer/songwriter, poet
Christena Graves, singer
Sara Groves, singer/songwriter
Amanda Haley, biblical archaeologist/editor
Charlie Hall, singer/songwriter
Kelly Hall, editor/poet
Justin Hyde, pastor/author
E. Chad Karger, counselor/author, pastor
Greg LaFollette, musician/songwriter
Phuc Luu, chaplain/adjunct instructor
Christian McCabe, pastor/artist
Donald Miller, author
Sean Palmer, pastor
Jonathan Hal Reynolds, poet
Robbie Seay, singer/songwriter
Allison Smythe, poet
Leonard Sweet, author
Phyllis Tickle, author/icon
Lauren Winner, lecturer/author
Seth Woods, singer/songwriter
Dieter Zander, pastor/author

Scholars

Biblical and theological scholars for *The Voice* include:

David Capes, PhD, department chair/professor
Alan Culpepper, PhD, dean/professor
Creig Marlowe, PhD, dean/professor
Peter H. Davids, PhD, pastor/professor
Jack Wisdom, JD, lawyer
Nancy de Claissé Walford, PhD, professor
Darrell Bock, PhD, professor
Dave Garber, PhD, professor
Joseph Blair, ThD, professor

Kenneth Waters, Sr., PhD, professor
Peter Rhea Jones, Sr., PhD, pastor/professor
Troy Miller, PhD, professor
Felisi Sorgwe, PhD, pastor/professor

Artists

Art and images will be incorporated into many of the products that will provide a visual reference, source of meditation, and convey the splendor of God's story that cannot be captured in words. The first book, *The Last Eyewitness: The Final Week* contains numerous illustrations by Rob Pepper, an accomplished British artist.

Musicians

The passages meant for use in worship are being set to music with a number of music albums planned. The recordings themselves are experiences of collaboration and worship. A large studio was selected to allow up to 20 musicians to perform live, creating a truly dynamic sound. Most of the featured artists participated in many of the songs, making a diverse and rich sound. The spirit of the retelling of the story found in **The Voice** comes through in this unique collection of songs in a variety of styles and moods. The first CD, *Songs from the Voice, Vol. 1*, contains 13 original songs inspired by selected psalms from **The Voice.** The second CD, *Songs from the Voice, Vol. 2*, features music drawn from the same Scripture selections as *Handel's Messiah* and the unique retelling about Messiah in **The Voice**. The featured artists are:

Derek Webb	Jill Phillips with	Jill Paquette
The Robbie Seay Band	Waterdeep	Andrew Peterson
Jami Smith	Tyler Burkum	Steven Delopoulos
Sandra McCracken	Tara Leigh Cobble	Lori Chaffer
Seth Woods	Kendall Payne	Don Chaffer
Sara Groves	Andrew Osenga	
Maeve	Matt Wertz	

A Final Word

These times of transition in which we find ourselves have been described in many ways. It is widely agreed that both our secular and religious cultures—

from the most liberal to the most conservative—have been deeply affected by a mind-set labeled "modern," and we now are grappling with the appearance of a new cultural ethos often called "postmodern." This transition has many dimensions: philosophical, artistic, technological, social, moral, economic, political, and theological. It is no surprise that in times of transition like these, fresh attention needs to be paid to how we translate, study, understand, teach, apply, and proclaim the vital message of the Scriptures.

During this unique time in the life of the church of Christ, there seems to be a change as to how we as the body of believers worship, fellowship, and communicate the truths of the gospel. *The Voice* appears at the point of impact where the modern church, with its tradition and stability, collides with the developing church of the future. We are working to help the church move through these changes and to focus its attention on God's Word. In reality, *The Voice* is the product of a community of believers seeking to bring alive the story of the Bible. The goal is to reinvigorate followers of Christ with the Scriptures. Together we all are weaving together our talents to retell the story and create tools to use with the narrative communication of the Bible. Together we are rediscovering the story of the Bible.

Introduction

This book lives up to my greatest hopes that the Scriptures have the power to breathe new life into every generation. The Bible is as diverse as it is authoritative. Our canon is an anthology of unique and divinely inspired literature that must be translated with great care for the spirit, meaning, and literary style of each unique book. Previous generations have skillfully accepted the task of translation and given birth to wonderful translations and paraphrases. But until this project each Bible has carried an overt bias for homogeneity that is considered the status quo of modernity. The time has come for a rare collaboration between artists, poets, writers, pastors, and scholars that will celebrate the true literary diversity of the Hebrew and Christian Scriptures.

There is no book in the Bible that compares in any way with the Book of Acts. It stands alone among all the narratives as a supernatural action-adventure. If this story were ever told on the silver screen, it would require actors of tremendous strength and presence to fill the sandals of Peter (for example, Bono) and Paul (for example, Russell Crowe). Brian McLaren has retold this spiritual adventure with the kind of power and grace that it deserves, and we have adapted his work to read like a screenplay.

Because of the importance of understanding the historical context in reading of the emergence of the first church, we selected a number of pastors and scholars to offer insight and to guide our reading. I am grateful to David Capes, Robert Creech, Greg Garrett, Tim Keel, Evan Lauer, and Chuck Smith, Jr., for their profound insight into this book.

It is also amazing to consider the impact this book has in radically different contexts that help to shape the values of the church. So I asked two of my very dear friends to reflect on places in this book that speak directly to their work.

1) Andrew Jones is a true postmodern prophet whose love for the gospel allows him to be heard equally by denominational leaders and kids who find their home on the streets of Haight and Asbury in San Francisco. If you do not already follow his daily reflections at

tallskinnykiwi.com, you will likely bookmark his blog after reading his reflections on the important shift to embrace Gentiles as true followers of God.

2) Kerry Shook is pastor of Fellowship of The Woodlands, a young mega-church in a north Houston suburb. His church has experienced amazing growth. Kerry and his wife, Chris, founded Fellowship of The Woodlands with eight people in 1993. In twelve years the church has grown to 13,000 in average attendance each Sunday. Kerry is recognized for his creative, practical, and relevant ministry. Fellowship of The Woodlands has been featured on Fox, NBC, and PBS. Kerry examines the lessons learned in Acts for a rapidly growing church from the perspective of a mega-church pastor.

So get ready to experience the supernatural power of God, public beatings, the beauty of true sharing, Christian community, imprisonments, powerful sermons, martyrdom, shipwreck, and almost everything in between. It's all here, it's all true, and it's anything but boring.

— Chris Seay

Section One // **The Dust Off Their Feet**

CONTINUING THE JOURNEY

¹To *a lover of God,* Theophilus:

In my first book I recounted the events of Jesus' life—His actions, His teachings—²·³*from the beginning of His life* until He was taken up into heaven. After His great suffering *and vindication,* He showed His apostles that He was alive—appearing to them repeatedly over a period of 40 days, giving them many convincing proofs of His resurrection. As before, He spoke constantly of the kingdom of God. During these appearances, He had instructed His chosen messengers through the Holy Spirit, ⁴prohibiting them from leaving Jerusalem, but rather requiring them to wait there until they received what He called "the promise of the Father."

Jesus | This is what you heard Me teach—⁵that just as John ritually cleansed* people with water, so you will be washed with the Holy Spirit very soon.

*S*cripture doesn't preserve Jesus' teachings during those mysterious meetings with the apostles after His death. We can only imagine the joy, curiosity, and amazement of the disciples as they hung on every word. What we do know is that His presence proved the reality of His bodily resurrection beyond any doubt and that He primarily wanted to talk to them about the kingdom of God. These words were

---

1:5 Literally, immersed, in a rite of initiation and purification

undoubtedly intended to prepare each of them for this journey, a journey with a clear destination in sight—the kingdom of God.

The kingdom of God is not a place, a belief system, a government, or a work of fiction—it's not even the heavenly kingdom. The kingdom of God is the rule of God in the hearts of His people. God is creating more than just the church out of this ragtag group of Christ-followers. He is birthing the kingdom of God, and the Holy Spirit is the midwife.

⁶When they had gathered *just outside Jerusalem at the Mount of Olives,* they asked Jesus,

Disciples | Is now the time, Lord—the time when You will reestablish Your kingdom in our land of Israel?

Jesus | ⁷The Father, on His own authority, has determined the ages and epochs of history, but you have not been given this knowledge. ⁸*Here's the knowledge you need:* you will receive power when the Holy Spirit comes on you. And you will be My witnesses, first here in Jerusalem, then beyond to Judea and Samaria, and finally to the farthest places on earth.

⁹As He finished this commission, He began to rise from the ground before their eyes until the clouds obscured Him from their vision. ¹⁰The apostles realized two men in white robes were standing among them.

Two Men | ¹¹You Galileans, why are you standing here staring up into the sky? This Jesus who is leaving you and

ascending to heaven will return in the same way you
see Him departing.

¹²Then the disciples returned to Jerusalem—their short journey
from the Mount of Olives was an acceptable Sabbath Day's walk.

¹³⁻¹⁴Back in the city, they went to the room where they were stay-
ing—a second-floor room. This whole group devoted themselves to
constant prayer with one accord: Peter, John, James, Andrew, Philip,
Thomas, Bartholomew, Matthew, James (son of Alphaeus), Simon (the
Zealot), Judas (son of James), a number of women including Mary
(Jesus' mother), and some of Jesus' brothers.

¹⁵As the disciples prayed, Peter stood among the group of about 120
people and made this proposal:

> **Peter |** ¹⁶⁻¹⁷My friends, everything in the Hebrew Scriptures
> had to be fulfilled, including what the Holy Spirit
> foretold through David about Judas. *As you know,* Judas
> was one of us and participated in our ministry until
> he guided the authorities to arrest Jesus. ¹⁸(He was
> paid handsomely for his betrayal, and he bought a field
> with the blood money. But he died on that land—
> falling so that his abdomen burst and his internal
> organs gushed out. ¹⁹News of this death spread to
> everyone in Jerusalem, so Judas's property is known as
> Hakeldama, which means "field of blood.") ²⁰In this way,
> one of *David's* psalms was fulfilled: "May their camps
> be bleak, with not one left in any tent."* But the psalm

1:20 Psalm 69:25-26

also includes these words: "Let his position of over-sight be given to another."* ²¹So we need to determine his replacement from among the men who have been with us during all of the Lord Jesus' travels among us—²²from His ritual cleansing* by John until His ascension. We need someone to join us as a witness of Jesus' resurrection.

²³The group put forward two men: Joseph (who was also known as Barsabbas or Justus) and Matthias.

Disciples | ²⁴Lord, You know everyone's heart. Make it clear to us which of these two is Your choice ²⁵to take on this ministry as an apostle, replacing Judas who went his own way to his own destination.

²⁶Then they drew lots, and the lot fell to Matthias, so he was added to the 11 apostles *to reconstitute the twelve.*

*T*he Creator of heaven and earth is orchestrating a redemptive story that will radically change the course of history. The most significant supernatural event in the history of this newly formed church will be the filling of the Holy Spirit. Through the Holy Spirit, God will direct the church's growth. But how did the early church make important decisions before the Holy Spirit descended on them?

With much thought and prayer?

1:20 Psalm 109:8
1:22 Literally, immersion, an act of repentance

By a carefully appointed committee?

With a democratic vote?

No. They left their decisions up to the providential leading of God. They called it "drawing lots." To seek God's direction, Joseph and Matthias most likely wrote their names on scraps; then someone drew the replacement's name out of a bag. What seems to us like a 50/50 chance was, in fact, God's way of imparting His will. You see, the disciples weren't putting their faith in "chance." They were putting their faith in a God who lives. And this living God wasn't distant; He was a player in their lives, active when His people sought Him and His will. They believed that God directed the process, start to finish, and determined whose name was drawn to join the eleven. When they drew lots, these early believers were using a centuries-old method to discern God's will. But with the filling of the Holy Spirit, the communication from God became more direct, and the drawing of lots was obsolete.

Acts 2

A TASTE OF THE KINGDOM

¹When the holy day of Pentecost came *50 days after Passover*, they were gathered together in one place.

Picture yourself among the disciples: ²A sound roars from the sky without warning, the roar of a violent wind, and the whole house where you are gathered reverberates with the sound. ³Then a flame appears, dividing into smaller flames and spreading from one person to the next. ⁴All the apostles are filled with the Holy Spirit and begin speaking in languages they've never spoken, as the Spirit empowers them.

⁵*Because of the holiday,* there were devoted Jews staying as pilgrims in Jerusalem from every nation under the sun. ⁶They heard the sound, and a crowd gathered. They were amazed because each of them could hear the group speaking in their native languages. ⁷They were shocked and amazed by this.

Pilgrims | Just a minute. Aren't all of these people Galileans? ⁸How in the world do we all hear our native languages being spoken? ⁹*Look*—there are Parthians *here*, and Medes, Elamites, Mesopotamians, and Judeans, residents of Cappadocia, Pontus, and Asia, ¹⁰Phrygians and Pamphylians, Egyptians and Libyans from Cyrene, Romans including both Jews by birth and converts, ¹¹Cretans, and Arabs. We're each, in our own languages, hearing these people talk about God's powerful deeds.

¹²Their amazement became confusion as they wondered,

Pilgrims | What does this mean?

Skeptics | ¹³It doesn't mean anything. They're all drunk on some fresh wine!

*N*o matter who you were or what you may have seen, this miraculous sign of God's kingdom would have astounded you. The followers of Jesus were not known as people who drank too much wine with breakfast, but this unusual episode required some kind of explanation. Unfortunately, we can't comprehend or express what transpired on Pentecost. But this was not a novelty performance; rather, it was a taste of the kingdom of God.

¹⁴As the twelve stood together, Peter shouted to the crowd,

Peter | Men of Judea and all who are staying here in Jerusalem, listen. I want you to understand: ¹⁵these people aren't drunk as you may think. Look, it's only nine o'clock in the morning! ¹⁶*No, this isn't drunkenness; this is the fulfillment of the prophecy of Joel. ¹⁷Hear what God says!*

In the last days, I will offer My Spirit to humanity as a libation.
Your children will boldly speak *the word of the Lord.*

Young warriors will see visions, and your elders will
dream dreams.

[18]Yes, in those days I shall offer My Spirit to all servants,
Both male and female, [and they will boldly speak the
word of the Lord].

[19]And in the heaven above and on the earth below,
I shall give signs *of impending judgment*: blood, fire, and
clouds of smoke.

[20]The sun will become a void of darkness, and the moon
will become blood.

Then the great and dreadful day of the Lord will arrive,

[21]And everyone who pleads using the name of the Lord
Will be liberated *into God's freedom and peace*.*

[22]All of you Israelites, listen to my message: it's about
Jesus of Nazareth, a Man whom God authenticated for
you by performing in your presence powerful deeds,
wonders, and signs through Him, just as you yourselves
know. [23]This *Man, Jesus*, who came into your hands by
God's sure plan and advanced knowledge, you nailed to
a cross and killed in collaboration with lawless Gentiles.
[24]But God raised Jesus and unleashed Him from the ago-
nizing birth-pains of death, for death could not possibly
keep Jesus in its power. [25]David spoke *of Jesus'
resurrection*, saying:

The Lord is ever present with me. I will not live in
fear or abandon my calling because He guides my

right hand. [26]My heart is glad; my soul rejoices; my body is safe. Who could want for more? [27]You will not abandon me to experience the suffering of a miserable afterlife. Nor leave me to rot alone. [28]Instead, You direct me on a path that leads to a beautiful life. As I walk with You the pleasures are never-ending, and I know true joy and contentment.*

[29]My fellow Israelites, I can say without question that David our ancestor died and was buried, and his tomb is with us today. [30]*David wasn't speaking of himself;* he was speaking as a prophet. *He saw with prophetic insight* that God had made a solemn promise to him: God would put one of his descendants on His throne. [31]Here's what David was seeing in advance; here's what David was talking about—the Messiah, the Liberating King, would be resurrected. *Think of David's words about* Him not being abandoned to the place of the dead nor being left to decay in the grave. [32]*He was talking about* Jesus, the One God has raised, whom all of us have seen with our own eyes and announce to you today. [33]Since Jesus has been lifted to the right hand of God—*the highest place of authority and power*—and since Jesus has received the promise of the Holy Spirit from the Father, He has now poured out what you have seen and heard here today. [34]*Remember:* David couldn't have been speaking of himself rising to the heavens when he said, "The Lord God said to my Lord, the King,

³⁵"Sit here at My right hand, in the place of honor and power, and I will gather Your enemies together, lead them in on hands and knees, and You will rest Your feet on their backs.'"*

³⁶Everyone in Israel should now realize with certainty *what God has done*: God has made Jesus both Lord and Liberating King—this same Jesus whom you crucified.

³⁷When the people heard this, their hearts were pierced and they said to Peter and his fellow apostles,

Pilgrims | Our brothers, what should we do?

Peter | ³⁸Reconsider your lives; change your direction. Participate in the ceremonial washing* in the name of Jesus the Liberating King. Then your sins will be forgiven, and the gift of the Holy Spirit will be yours. ³⁹For the promise *of the Spirit* is for you, for your children, for all people—even those considered outsiders and outcasts—the Lord our God invites everyone to come to Him. Let God liberate you from this decaying culture!

Peter was pleading and offering many logical reasons to believe. ⁴¹Whoever made a place for his message in their hearts received the ceremonial washing*; in fact, that day alone, about 3,000 people joined the disciples.

2:35 Psalm 110:1
2:38 Literally, immersion, a rite of initiation and purification
2:41 Literally, immersion, a rite of initiation and purification

⁴²The community continually committed themselves to learning what the apostles taught them, gathering for fellowship, breaking the bread, and praying. ⁴³Everyone felt a sense of awe because the apostles were doing many signs and wonders among them. ⁴⁴There was an intense sense of togetherness among all who believed; they shared all their material possessions in trust. ⁴⁵They sold any possessions and goods *that did not benefit the community* and used the money to help everyone in need. ⁴⁶They were unified as they worshiped at the temple day after day. In homes, they broke bread and shared meals with glad and generous hearts. ⁴⁷The new disciples praised God, and they enjoyed the goodwill of all the people of the city. Day after day the Lord added to their number everyone who was experiencing liberation.

*A*lthough this young and thriving church had no political influence, property, fame, or wealth, it was powerful. Its power was centered in living the gospel. The people valued one another more than any possessions. They came together as a large, passionate, healthy family where it was natural to pray and share all of life together. The kingdom of God was blossoming on earth as these lovers of God embraced the teachings of Christ. The church has since lost much of the beauty and appeal we see in Acts. It has become concerned with a desire for material possessions, cultural influence, and large congregations.

WHY ARE YOU SO AMAZED?

¹*One day* at three o'clock in the afternoon, a customary time for daily prayer, Peter and John walked to the temple. ²Some people were carrying in a man who had been paralyzed since birth. Every day they brought him to a place near the Beautiful Gate (one of the temple entrances) so he could beg for money from people entering *to worship*. ³He saw Peter and John coming and asked them for a contribution. ⁴Peter gazed intensely at him—so did John.

> **Peter** | Look at us.

⁵The man looked up at them, assuming they were about to give him some money.

> **Peter** | ⁶I want to give you something, but I don't have any silver or gold. Here's what I can offer you: stand up and walk in the name of Jesus of Nazareth, the Liberating King.

⁷Then Peter took the man's right hand and lifted him to his feet. Instantly, the man's feet and ankles grew strong. ⁸He jumped and walked, accompanying Peter and John into the temple where he walked, jumped for joy, and shouted praises to God. ⁹⁻¹¹A crowd ran to the commotion, and they gathered around this man in an open area called Solomon's Porch. There he was, standing on his own two feet,

holding on to Peter and John. They knew exactly who he was—the beggar they passed at the Beautiful Gate every day. Everyone was absolutely amazed at this wonderful miracle; they were speechless, stunned.

Peter
(to the crowd)

[12]Why are you so amazed, my fellow Israelites? Why are you staring at my friend and me as though we did this miracle through our own power or made this fellow walk by our own holiness? [13]*We didn't do this—God did!* The God of Abraham, the God of Isaac, the God of Jacob—the God of our ancestors has glorified Jesus, God's servant. The same Jesus whom you betrayed and rejected in front of Pilate, even though Pilate was going to release Him. [14]He was the Holy and Righteous One, but you rejected Him and asked for a murderer to be released to you instead. [15]*You not only rejected Him,* but you killed Him—the very Author of life! But God raised Jesus from the dead, whom my friend John and I have seen with our own eyes. [16]So that's how this miracle happened: we have faith in the name of Jesus, and Jesus is the power that made this man strong—this man who is known to all of you. It is faith in Jesus that has given this man his complete health here today, in front of all of you.

[17]Listen, friends, I know you didn't fully realize what you were doing *when you rejected and betrayed Jesus.* I know that you, and your rulers as well, were acting in ignorance. [18]God was at work in all this, fulfilling what

He had predicted through all the prophets—that His Liberating King would suffer. [19]So now you need to rethink everything and turn to God so your sins will be forgiven and a new day can dawn, days of refreshing times flowing from the Lord. [20]Then God may send the Liberating King—Jesus, whom God has chosen for you. [21]He is in heaven now and must remain there until the day of universal restoration comes—the restoration which in ancient times God announced through the holy prophets. [22]Moses, *for example,* said, "The Lord your God will raise up from among your people a prophet who will be like me. You must listen to Him. [23]And whoever does not listen to His words [will be completely uprooted from among the people]."*

[24]*It wasn't just Moses who predicted what is happening these days.* Every prophet, from Samuel through all of his successors, agreed. [25]You are the descendants of these prophets, and you are the people of God's covenant to your ancestors. God's word to Abraham includes you: "Because of your descendants, all the Gentile nations of the earth will be blessed."* [26]So when God raised up His Servant, God sent Him first to you, to begin blessing you by calling you to change your path from evil ways *to God's ways.*

3:23 Deuteronomy 18:15, 18-19
3:25 Genesis 22:18 and Genesis 26:4

WITH A BOLDNESS NOT HIS OWN

¹The conversation continued *for a few hours there in Solomon's Porch.* Suddenly, the head of the temple police and some members of the Sadducean party interrupted Peter and John. ²They were annoyed because Peter and John were *enthusiastically* teaching that in Jesus, resurrection of the dead is possible—*an idea the Sadducees completely rejected.* ³So they arrested Peter, John, *and the man who was healed* and kept them in jail overnight. ⁴*But during these few afternoon hours between the man's miraculous healing and their arrest,* Peter and John already had convinced about 5,000 more people to believe their message about Jesus!

*T*he support for this band of Christ-followers was growing by the day. What was it about this early incarnation of Christianity that was so appealing? Was it a less tainted depiction of the gospel, or were the people more receptive? In the centuries since the first church, the term "Christian" often became synonymous with hatred, greatly reducing its appeal.

⁵The next morning, *the Jewish leaders*—their officials, elders, and scholars—called a meeting in Jerusalem ⁶presided over by Annas (the patriarch of the ruling priestly clan), along with Caiaphas *(his son-in-law),* John, Alexander, and other members of their clan. ⁷They made their prisoners stand in the middle of the assembly and questioned them.

Jewish Leaders	Who gave you the authority to create that spectacle in the temple yesterday?

Peter *(filled with the Spirit)*	[8]Rulers and elders of the people, [9]yesterday a good deed was done. Someone who was sick was healed. If you're asking us how this happened, [10]I want all of you and all of the people of Israel to know this man standing in front of you—obviously in good health— was healed by the authority of Jesus, the Liberating King from Nazareth. This is the same Jesus whom you crucified and whom God raised from the dead. [11]He is "the stone that the builders rejected [who] has become the very stone that holds up the entire foundation"* *on which a new temple is being built.* [12]There is no one else who can rescue us, and there is no other name under heaven given to any human by whom we may be rescued.

[13]Now the leaders were surprised and confused. They looked at Peter and John and realized they were *typical peasants*—uneducated, utterly ordinary fellows—with extraordinary confidence. The leaders recognized them as companions of Jesus, [14]then they turned their attention to the third man standing beside them—recently lame, now standing tall and healthy. What could they say in response to all this?

[15]*Because they were at a loss about what to say or do,* they excused the prisoners so the council could deliberate in private.

4:11 Psalm 118:22

Jewish Leaders | ¹⁶What do we do with these fellows? Anyone who lives in Jerusalem will know an unexplainable sign has been performed through these two preachers. We can't deny their story. ¹⁷The best we can do is try to keep it from spreading. So let's warn them to stop speaking to anybody in this name.

¹⁸The leaders brought the prisoners back in and prohibited them from doing any more speaking or teaching in the name of Jesus. ¹⁹Peter and John *listened quietly and then* replied,

Peter and John | You are the judges here, so we'll leave it up to you to judge whether it is right in the sight of God to obey your commands or God's. ²⁰⁻²¹*But one thing we can tell you:* we cannot possibly restrain ourselves from speaking about what we have seen and heard with our own eyes and ears.

The council threatened them again, but finally let them go because public opinion strongly supported Peter and John and this man who had received this miraculous sign. ²²He was over 40 years old, *so his situation was known to many people,* and they couldn't help but glorify God for his healing.

²³Peter and John, upon their release, went right to their friends and told the story—including the warning from the council. ²⁴The whole community responded with this prayer to God:

Community of Believers

God, our King, You made the heaven and the earth and the sea and everything they contain. ²⁵You are the One who, by the Holy Spirit, spoke through our ancestor David, Your servant, with these words: "Why did the nations rage? Why did they imagine useless things? ²⁶The kings of the earth took their stand; their rulers assembled in opposition against the Lord and His Liberating King."* ²⁷This is exactly what has happened among us, here in this city. *The Gentile ruler* Pontius Pilate and *the Jewish ruler* Herod, along with their respective peoples, have assembled in opposition to Your holy servant Jesus, the One You chose. ²⁸They have done whatever Your hand and plan predetermined should happen. ²⁹And now, Lord, take note of their intimidations *intended to silence us*. Grant us, Your servants, the courageous confidence we need to go ahead and proclaim Your message ³⁰while You reach out Your hand to heal people, enabling us to perform signs and wonders through the name of Your holy servant Jesus.

³¹They finished their prayer, and immediately the whole place where they had gathered began to shake. All the disciples were filled with the Holy Spirit, and they began speaking God's message with courageous confidence.

*T*he Holy Spirit changed everyone and everything. If there is any doubt about the power of the Spirit, just take a look at Peter. When Christ

4:26 Psalm 2:12

was captured, Peter cowered in fear that he might be fingered as a man who loved Jesus. Now this same man is preaching, healing, and pointing his finger in the face of Jewish officials who have captured him and John. With a boldness that is not his own, he blames them for the death of Jesus the Liberating King and does not cower at their show of violence.

[32]*During those days,* the entire community of believers was deeply united in heart and soul to such an extent that they stopped claiming private ownership of their possessions. Instead, they held everything in common. [33]The apostles with great power gave their eyewitness reports of the resurrection of the Lord Jesus. Everyone was surrounded by an extraordinary grace. [34]Not a single person in the community was in need because those who had been affluent sold their houses or lands and brought the proceeds [35]to the apostles. The apostles then distributed the funds to individuals according to their needs. [36-37]One fellow, a Cyprian Levite named Joseph, earned a nickname *because of his generosity* in selling a field and bringing the money to the apostles *in this way.* From that time on, the apostles called him Barnabas, which means "son of encouragement."

*T*his portrait of the early church as an unselfish community is captivating and inspiring. But, how does this translate into future cultures? How do we, in our time, respond as they did in theirs?

How do we speak boldy?

How do we bring healing and miracles in God's name?

How do we join together with one heart and mind?

How do we relinquish our possessions?

Acts 5

FRAUD IN THE COMMUNITY

¹⁻²*The life of the community was wonderful in those days, but it wasn't perfect.*
Once a man named Ananias, with his wife Sapphira fully cooperating,
committed fraud. He sold some property and kept some of the proceeds,
but he pretended to make a full donation to the apostles.

Peter | ³Ananias, have you allowed Satan to influence your lies
to the Holy Spirit and hold back some of the money?
⁴Look, it was your property before you sold it, and the
money was all yours after you sold it. Why have you
concocted this scheme in your heart? You weren't just
lying to us; you were lying to God.

⁵Ananias heard these words and immediately dropped to the ground,
dead; fear overcame all those who heard of the incident. ⁶Some young men
came, wrapped the body, and buried it immediately. ⁷About three hours
had passed when Sapphira arrived. She had no idea what had happened.

Peter | ⁸Did you sell the land for such-and-such a price?

Sapphira | Yes, that was the price.

Peter | ⁹Why did the two of you conspire to test the Spirit of
the Lord? Do you hear those footsteps outside? Those
are the young men who just buried your husband, and
now they will carry you out as well.

[10]She—like her husband—immediately fell dead at Peter's feet. The young men came in and carried her corpse outside and buried it beside her husband. [11]The whole church was terrified by this story, as were others who heard it.

*I*n these formative days, God chose to send some strong messages about His work in the church: the power to heal, the beauty of life in the Spirit, and His hatred for arrogant religion. If God had not rebuked the married couple who chose to make a show of their supposed generosity, Christianity would have drifted in the wrong direction. The Jewish leaders were using religion as a means to gain power and increase their reputations. The teachings of the true Messiah, Jesus, lead us down a path toward the kingdom of God rather than toward our own advancement. God chose to expose these bad motives quickly, so that the church throughout history would give out of pure motives rather than out of a desire to appear righteous.

[12]*Those were amazing days*—with many signs and wonders being performed through the apostles among the people. The church would gather as a unified group in Solomon's Porch [13]enjoying great respect by the people of the city—though most people wouldn't risk publicly affiliating with them. [14]Even so, record numbers of believers—both men and women—were added to the Lord. [15]*The church's popularity was so great that* when Peter walked down the street, people would carry out their sick relatives hoping his shadow would fall on some of them as he passed. [16]Even people from towns surrounding Jerusalem would come, bringing others who were sick or tormented by unclean spirits, all of whom were cured.

[17]*Of course, this popularity elicited a response:* the high priest and his affiliates in the Sadducean party were jealous, [18]so they arrested the apostles and put them in the public prison. [19]But that night, an angel of the Lord opened the doors of the prison and led them to freedom.

> **Angel** | [20]Go to the temple, and stand up to tell the people the whole message about this way of life from Jesus.

[21]At dawn they did as they were told; they returned to their teaching in the temple.

Meanwhile, the council of Jewish elders was gathering—convened by the high priest and his colleagues. They sent the temple police to the prison to have the apostles brought *for further examination,* [22]but, of course, the temple police soon realized the apostles weren't there. They returned and reported,

> **Temple Police** | [23]The prison was secure and locked, and the guards were standing in front of the doors, but when we unlocked the doors, the cell was empty.

[24]The captain of the temple police and the senior priests were completely mystified when they heard this. They had no idea what had happened. [25]Just then, someone arrived with this news:

> **Messenger** | You know those men you put in prison last night? *Well, they're free.* At this moment *they're at it again,* teaching our people in the temple!

[26]The temple police—this time, accompanied by their captain—rushed over to the temple and brought the apostles to the council. They were

careful not to use violence, because the people were so supportive of the apostles that the police feared being stoned by the crowd *if they were too rough.* [27]Once again the apostles stood before the council. The high priest began the questioning.

High Priest | [28]Didn't we give you strict orders to stop teaching in this name? But here you are, spreading your teaching throughout Jerusalem. And you are determined to blame us for this Man's death.

Peter and the Apostles | [29]If we have to choose between obedience to God and obedience to any human authority, then we must obey God. [30]The God of our ancestors raised Jesus from death. You killed Jesus by hanging Him on a tree, [31]but God has lifted Him high, to God's own right hand, as the Prince, as the Liberator. God intends to bring Israel to a radical rethinking of our lives and to a complete forgiveness of our sins. [32]We are witnesses to these things. There is another witness too—the Holy Spirit— whom God has given to all who choose to obey Him.

[33]*Peter's speech didn't go over very well.* The council was furious and would have killed them, [34]but Gamaliel, a Pharisee in the council respected as a teacher of the Hebrew Scriptures, stood up and ordered the apostles to be sent out *so the council could confer privately.*

Gamaliel | [35]Fellow Jews, you need to act with great care in your treatment of these fellows. [36]Remember when a man named Theudas rose to notoriety? He claimed to be somebody important, and he attracted about 400 followers. But when he was killed, his entire movement disintegrated and nothing came of it. [37]After him came Judas, that Galilean fellow, at the time of the census. He also attracted a following, but when he died, his entire movement fell apart. [38]So here's my advice: in this case, just let these men go. Ignore them. If this is just another movement arising from human enthusiasm, it will die out soon enough. [39]But then again, if God is in this, you won't be able to stop it—unless, of course, you're ready to fight against God!

[40]The council was convinced, so they brought the apostles back in. The apostles were flogged, again told not to speak in the name of Jesus, and then released.

[41]The apostles, as they left the council, *weren't discouraged at all. In fact*, they were filled with joy over being considered worthy to suffer disgrace for the sake of the His name. [42]And constantly, whether in public, in the temple, or in their homes, they kept teaching and proclaiming Jesus as the Liberating King.

*T*hese apostles inspire us with their passion to serve Jesus and advance the gospel in the face of torture and abuse. After a night in prison and a public flogging, they move forward with smiles on their faces. We are often crippled by mere criticism or the fear that we might be criticized. What would happen to the church if we embraced the boldness of the apostles and risked our own safety to see the captives rescued and the oppressed freed?

PROBLEMS IN THE KITCHEN

¹*Things were going so well,* and the number of disciples was growing. But a problem arose. The Greek-speaking believers became frustrated with the Hebrew-speaking believers. The Greeks complained that the Greek-speaking widows were being discriminated against in the daily distribution of food. ²The twelve convened the entire community of disciples.

The Twelve | We could solve this problem ourselves, but that wouldn't be right. We need to focus on proclaiming God's message, not on distributing food. ³So, friends, find seven respected men from the community of faith. These men should be full of the Holy Spirit and full of wisdom. Whomever you select we will commission to resolve this matter, ⁴so we can maintain our focus on praying and serving—*not meals*—but the message.

⁵The whole community—*Greek-speaking and Hebrew-speaking*—was very pleased with this plan, so they chose *seven men:* Stephen (a man full of faith and full of the Holy Spirit), Philip, Prochorus, Nicanor, Timon, Parmenas, and Nicolas (a Greek-speaking convert from Antioch). ⁶These men were presented to the apostles, who then prayed for them and commissioned them by laying their hands on them. ⁷The message of God continued to spread, and the number of disciples continued to increase significantly there in Jerusalem. Even priests in large numbers became obedient to the faith.

⁸Stephen continually overflowed with extraordinary grace and power, and he was able to perform a number of miraculous signs and wonders in public view. ⁹But eventually, a group arose to oppose Stephen and the message to which his signs and wonders pointed. (These men were from a group called the Free Synagogue and included Cyrenians, Alexandrians, Cilicians, and Asians.) ¹⁰The Holy Spirit gave Stephen such wisdom in responding to their arguments that they were humiliated; ¹¹in retaliation, they spread a vicious rumor: "We heard Stephen speak blasphemies against Moses and God."

¹²Their rumor prompted an uprising that included common people, religious officials, and scholars. They surprised Stephen, grabbed him, and hauled him before the council. ¹³They convinced some witnesses to give false testimony.

False Witnesses | This fellow constantly degrades the holy temple and mocks our holy Law. ¹⁴With our own ears we've heard him say this Jesus fellow, this Nazarene *he's always talking about,* will actually destroy the holy temple and will try to change the sacred customs we received from Moses.

¹⁵The entire council turned its gaze on Stephen to see how he would respond. They were shocked to see his face radiant *with peace*—as if he were an angel.

THE GREATEST OF ALL FAILURES

High Priest | *¹What do you have to say for yourself?* Are these accusations accurate?

Stephen | ²Brothers, fathers, please listen to me. Our glorious God revealed Himself to our common ancestor Abraham, when he lived far away in Mesopotamia before he immigrated to Haran. ³God gave him this command: "Leave your country. Leave your family and your inheritance. Move into unknown territory, where I will show you a new homeland."* ⁴First, he left Chaldea *in southern Mesopotamia* and settled in Haran until his father died. Then God led him still farther from his original home—until he settled here, in our land. ⁵*But at that point,* God still hadn't given him any of this land as his permanent possession—not even the footprint under his sandal actually belonged to him yet. But God did give Abraham a promise—a promise that yes, someday, the entire land would indeed belong to him and his descendants. *Of course, this promise was all the more amazing because* at that moment, Abraham had no descendants at all.

⁶God said that Abraham's descendants would first live in a foreign country as resident aliens, *as refugees,* for 400 years. During this time, they would be

---

enslaved and treated horribly. *But that would not be the end of the story.* [7]God promised, "I will judge the nation that enslaves them,"* and "I will bring them to this mountain to serve Me."* [8]God gave him the covenant ritual of circumcision *as a sign of His sacred promise.* When Abraham fathered his son, Isaac, he performed this ritual of circumcision on the eighth day. Then Isaac fathered Jacob, and Jacob fathered the twelve patriarchs.

[9]The patriarchs were jealous of their brother Joseph, so they sold him as a slave. Even so, God was with him, [10]and time after time, God rescued Joseph from whatever trials befell him. God gave Joseph the favor and wisdom to overcome each adversity and eventually to win the confidence and respect of his captors, including Pharaoh, the king of Egypt himself. So Pharaoh entrusted his whole nation and his whole household to Joseph's stewardship. [11]*Some time later,* a terrible famine spread through the entire region—from Canaan down to Egypt—and everyone suffered greatly. Our ancestors, living here in the region of Canaan, could find nothing to eat. [12]Jacob heard that Egypt had stores of grain, so he sent our forefathers, *his sons, to procure food* there. [13]Later, when they returned to Egypt a second time, Joseph revealed his true identity to them. He also told Pharaoh his family story.

[14-16]Joseph then invited his father Jacob and all his clan to come and live with him in Egypt. So Jacob came, along with 75 extended family members. After

7:7 Genesis 15:14
7:7 Exodus 3:12

their deaths, their remains were brought back to this land so they could be buried in the same tomb where Abraham *had buried Sarah* (he had purchased the tomb for a certain amount of silver from the family of Hamor in *the town of* Shechem).

[17]Still, God's promise to Abraham had not yet been fulfilled, but the time for that fulfillment was drawing very near. In the meantime, our ancestors living in Egypt rapidly multiplied. [18]Eventually a new king came to power—one who had not known Joseph *when he was the most powerful man in Egypt.* [19]This new leader *feared the growing population of our ancestors and* manipulated them for his own benefit, eventually seeking to control their population by forcing them to abandon their infants so they would die. [20]Into this horrible situation our ancestor Moses was born, and he was a beautiful child in God's eyes. He was raised for three months in his father's home, [21]and then he was abandoned *as the brutal regime required.* However, Pharaoh's daughter found, adopted, and raised him as her own son. [22]So Moses learned the culture and wisdom of the Egyptians and became a powerful man—both as an intellectual and as a leader. [23]When he reached the age of 40, his heart drew him to visit his kinfolk, our ancestors, the Israelites. [24]During his visit, he saw one of our people being wronged, and he took sides with our people by killing an Egyptian. [25]He thought his kinfolk would recognize him as their God-given liberator, but they didn't realize who he was and what he represented.

²⁶The next day Moses was walking among the Israelites again when he observed a fight—but this time, it was between two Israelites. He intervened and tried to reconcile the men. "You two are brothers," he said. "Why do you attack each other?" ²⁷But the aggressor pushed Moses away and responded *with contempt*: "Who made you our prince and judge? ²⁸Are you going to slay me *and hide my body* as you did with the Egyptian yesterday?"* ²⁹Realizing this murder had not gone unnoticed, he quickly escaped Egypt and lived as a refugee in the land of Midian. He *married there and* had two sons.

³⁰Forty more years passed. One day while Moses was in the desert near Mount Sinai, an angel appeared to him in the flames of a burning bush. ³¹The phenomenon intrigued Moses, and as he approached for a closer look, he heard a voice—the voice of the Lord: ³²"I am the God of your own fathers, the God of Abraham, Isaac, and Jacob."* This terrified Moses—he began to tremble and looked away in fear. ³³The voice continued: "Take off your sandals *and stand barefoot on the ground in My presence*, for this ground is holy ground. ³⁴I have avidly watched how My people are being mistreated by the Egyptians. I have heard their groaning at *the treatment of* their oppressors. I am descending *personally* to rescue them. So get up. I'm sending you to Egypt."*

³⁵*Now remember:* this was the same Moses who had been rejected by his kinfolk when they said, "Who

made you our prince and judge?" *This man, rejected by his own people,* was the one God had truly sent, commissioned by the angel who appeared in the bush, to be their leader and liberator.

³⁶*You remember what happened next.* Moses indeed led our ancestors to freedom, and he performed miraculous signs and wonders in Egypt, at the Red Sea, and in the wilderness over a period of 40 years. ³⁷This Moses promised our ancestors, "The Lord your God will raise up from among your people a Prophet who will be like me."* ³⁸This is the same one who led the people to Mount Sinai, where an angel spoke to him and our ancestors, and who received the living message of God to give to us.

³⁹But our ancestors still resisted. They again pushed Moses away and refused to follow him. In their hearts, they were ready to return to their former slavery in Egypt. ⁴⁰*While Moses was on the mountain communing with God,* they begged Aaron to make idols to lead them—*they actually preferred idols to following Moses in the way of the Lord.* "We have no idea what happened to this fellow, Moses, who brought us from Egypt,"* they said. ⁴¹So they made a calf as their new god, and they even sacrificed to it and celebrated an object they had fabricated *as if it were their God.*

⁴²*And you remember what God did next:* He let them go. He turned from them and let them follow their

---

idolatrous path—worshiping sun, moon, and stars just *as their unenlightened neighbors did.* The prophet *Amos* spoke for God about this horrible betrayal: "Did you offer Me sacrifices or give Me offerings during your 40-year wilderness journey, you Israelites? [43]*No, but* you have taken along your sacred tent for the worship of Moloch, and you honored the star of Rompha, your false god. So, if you want to worship your man-made images, you may do so—beyond Babylon."*

[44]Now recall that our ancestors had a sacred tent in the wilderness, the tent God directed Moses to build according to the pattern revealed to him. [45]When Joshua led our ancestors to dispossess the nations God drove out before them, our ancestors carried this sacred tent. It remained here in the land until the time of David. [46]David found favor with God and asked Him for permission to build a permanent structure *(rather than a portable tent)* to honor Him. [47]It was, of course, Solomon who actually built God's house. [48]Yet we all know the Most High God doesn't actually dwell in structures made by human hands, as the prophet *Isaiah* said, [49]"Since My throne is heaven and since My footstool is earth—what kind of structure can you build to contain Me? What man-made space could provide Me a resting place? asks the Lord. [50]Didn't I make all things with My own hand?"*

[51]You stubborn, stiff-necked people! Sure, you are

7:43 Amos 5:26-27
7:50 Isaiah 66:1-2

physically Jews, but you are no different from Gentiles in your hearts and ears! You are just like your ancestors, constantly fighting against the Holy Spirit. [52]Didn't your ancestors persecute the prophets? First, they killed those prophets who predicted the coming of the Just One, and now you have betrayed and murdered the Just One Himself! [53]Yes, you received the law as given by angels, but you haven't kept the law which you received.

[54]Upon hearing this, his audience could contain themselves no longer; they boiled in fury at Stephen; they clenched their jaws and ground their teeth. [55]*But Stephen didn't seem to notice. Instead of being filled with fear,* he was filled with the Holy Spirit. Gazing upward into heaven, he saw *something they couldn't see:* the glory of God, and Jesus standing at His right hand.

Stephen | [56]Look, I see the heavens opening! I see the Liberator standing at the right hand of God!

[57]At this, they covered their ears and started shouting. The whole crowd rushed at Stephen, converged on him, [58]dragged him out of the city, and stoned him.

They laid their coats at the feet of a young man named Saul, [59]while they were pelting Stephen with rocks.

Stephen | Lord Jesus, receive my spirit.

[60]Then he knelt in prayer, shouting at the top of his lungs,

Stephen | Lord, do not hold this evil against them.

Those were his final words; then he fell asleep *in death*.

*S*tephen's sermon is one of the most profound ever preached. He weaves together the story of the Jews and the life of Jesus. The point of the message is that God pursues us despite our constant failure. The assassination of Jesus is greatest of all of these failures.

Stephen affirms that through circumcision they have made themselves look like Jews, but their hearts and ears need circumcising as well. As you might expect, telling the Jewish leaders of the day to get their hearts and ears circumcised elicits a rather violent response. Stephen speaks the truth so that all might hear, including a man named Saul.

PHILIP'S GREAT ADVENTURE

¹⁻²Some devout men buried Stephen and mourned his passing with loud cries of grief. But Saul, *this young man who seemed to be supervising the whole violent event,* was pleased by Stephen's death. That very day, the *whole* church in Jerusalem began experiencing severe persecution. *All of the followers of Jesus*—except for the apostles themselves—fled to the countryside of Judea and Samaria *(the very places, you remember, where Jesus said His disciples would be His witnesses).* ³Young Saul went on a rampage—hunting the church, house after house, dragging both men and women to prison.

⁴All those who had been scattered *by the persecution* moved *from place to place, and wherever they went, they weren't afraid or silent.* Instead, they spread the message of Jesus.

⁵Philip, *for example,* headed north to the city of Samaria, and he told them the news of the Liberating King. ⁶The crowds were united in their desire to understand Philip's message. They not only listened with their ears, but they witnessed miraculous signs with their eyes. ⁷Unclean spirits cried out with loud screams as they were exorcised from people. Paralyzed people and lame people moved and walked in plain view. ⁸So the city was swept with joy.

⁹⁻¹¹There was a fellow named Simon who had a widespread and long-standing reputation as a magician in Samaria. Everyone—not just poor or uneducated people, but also the city's elite—paid him great respect. Because he had amazed them with his magic, they thought, "This is a

truly great man, full of the power of the God of Greatness." [12]But they were even more impressed with Philip as he proclaimed the good news of the kingdom of God and the name of Jesus the Liberating King. Both men and women received ceremonial washing*—[13]and even Simon himself became a believer. After his ceremonial washing* he shadowed Philip constantly, and he was as amazed as everyone else when he saw great and miraculous signs taking place.

[14]Meanwhile, word had reached the apostles in Jerusalem that the message of God was welcomed in Samaria—*a land of half-breeds and heretics in the minds of many Judeans*. The apostles sent Peter and John [15]to pray for the Samaritans. They were especially eager to see if the new believers would receive the Holy Spirit [16]because until this point they had been ceremonially washed* in the name of the Lord Jesus but had not experienced the Holy Spirit. [17]When Peter and John laid hands on the people, the Holy Spirit did indeed come upon them *all*.

[18]Simon *watched all this closely.* He saw the Holy Spirit coming to the people when the apostles laid hands on them. So he *came to Peter and John* and offered them money.

Simon | [19]I want to purchase this ability to confer the Holy Spirit on people through the laying on of my hands.

Peter | [20]May your silver rot right along with you, Simon! To think the Holy Spirit is a *magic trick* that can be procured with money! [21]You aren't even close to being ready for this kind of ministry; your heart is not right with God. [22]You need to turn from your past, and you

---

8:12 Literally, immersion, a rite of initiation and purification
8:13 Literally, immersion, a rite of initiation and purification
8:16 Literally, immersed, in a rite of initiation and purification

need to pray that the Lord will forgive the evil intent of your heart. ²³I can see deep bitterness has poisoned you, and wickedness has locked you in chains.

Simon | ²⁴Please—you must pray to the Lord for me. I don't want these terrible things to be true of me.

²⁵Peter and John preached to and talked *with the Samaritans* about the message of the Lord, and then they returned to Jerusalem, stopping in many other Samaritan villages along the way to proclaim the good news.

²⁶*During his time preaching in Samaria,* an angel brought this *short* message from the Lord to Philip:

Angel | Leave Samaria. Go south to the Jerusalem-Gaza road.

That was the whole message. It was especially unusual because this road runs through the middle of uninhabited desert. ²⁷But Philip got up, *left the excitement of Samaria,* and did as he was told to do. *Along this road, Philip saw a chariot in the distance.*

In the chariot was a dignitary from Ethiopia (the treasurer for Queen Candace), *an African man* who had been castrated. He had gone north to Jerusalem to worship at the Jewish temple, ²⁸and he was now *heading southwest* on his way home. He was seated in the chariot and was reading aloud from a scroll of the prophet Isaiah.

²⁹Philip received another prompting from the Holy Spirit:

Holy Spirit | Go over to the chariot and climb on board.

[30]So he started running until he was even with the chariot. Philip heard the Ethiopian reading aloud and recognized the words from the prophet Isaiah.

Philip | Do you understand the meaning of what you're reading?

The Ethiopian | [31]How can I understand it unless I have a mentor?

Then he invited Philip to sit in the chariot. [32]Here's the passage he was reading from the Hebrew Scriptures:

> Like a sheep, He was led to be slaughtered.
> Like a lamb about to be shorn of its wool, He was completely silent.
> [33]He was humiliated, and He received no justice.
> Who can describe His peers? *Who would treat Him this way?*
> For they snuffed out His life.*

The Ethiopian | [34]Here's my first question. Is the prophet describing his own situation, or is he describing someone else's *calamity*?

[35]That began a conversation in which Philip used the passage to explain the good news of Jesus. [36]Eventually, the chariot passed a body of water beside the road.

The Ethiopian | Since there is water here, is there anything that might prevent me from being ceremonially washed* *and identified as a disciple of Jesus*?

8:33 Isaiah 53:7-8
8:36 Literally, immersed, in a rite of initiation and purification

Philip | [³⁷If you believe in your heart that Jesus is the
          Liberating King, then nothing can stop you.

The Ethiopian said that he believed.]*

³⁸He commanded the charioteer to stop the horses. Then Philip and
the Ethiopian official walked together into the water. There Philip
washed him ceremonially,* *initiating him as a fellow disciple.* ³⁹When they
came out of the water, Philip was immediately caught up by the Holy
Spirit and taken from the sight of the Ethiopian, who climbed back
into his chariot and continued on his journey, overflowing with joy.
⁴⁰Philip found himself at a town called Azotus *(formerly the Philistine capital city of Ashdod, on the Mediterranean),* and from there he traveled north
again, proclaiming the good news in town after town until he came to
Caesarea.

8:37 The official may have been referring to the prohibition in Judaism from participating in temple worship
against men like himself, ones who had been castrated—a prohibition he would likely have encountered in this
very visit to Jerusalem. Verse 37 is omitted in the earliest manuscripts.
8:38 Literally, immersed, in a rite of initiation and purification

Acts 9

ON THE ROAD WITH SAUL

¹Back to Saul—this fuming, raging, hateful man who wanted to kill every last one of the Lord's disciples: he went to the high priest *in Jerusalem* ²for authorization to purge all the synagogues in Damascus of followers of the way of Jesus. His plan was to arrest and chain any of Jesus' followers—women as well as men—and transport them back to Jerusalem. ³He traveled north toward Damascus *with a group of companions.*

Imagine this: A light flashes from the sky around *you.* ⁴Saul falls to the ground at the sound of a Voice.

The Lord | Saul, Saul, why are you attacking Me?

Saul | ⁵Lord, who are You?

Then he hears these words—*shocking, unexpected words that will change his life forever—*

The Lord | I am Jesus. I am the One you are attacking. ⁶Get up.
　　　　　　Enter the city. You will learn there what you are to do.

⁷His other traveling companions just stand there, *paralyzed,* speechless because *they too* heard the Voice, but there is nobody in sight. ⁸Saul rises to his feet, his eyes wide-open, but he can't see a thing. So his companions lead *their* blind friend by the hand and take him into Damascus. ⁹He waits for three days—completely blind—and does not eat a bite or drink a drop of anything.

[10]Meanwhile, in Damascus a disciple named Ananias had a vision in which the Lord Jesus spoke to him.

Lord | Ananias.

Ananias | Here I am, Lord.

Lord | [11]Get up and go to Straight Boulevard. Go to the house of Judas and inquire about a man from Tarsus, Saul by name. He is praying *to Me at this very instant.* [12]He has had a vision—a vision of a man by your name who will come, lay hands on him, and heal his eyesight.

Ananias | [13]Lord, I know whom You're talking about. I've heard rumors about this fellow. He*'s an evil man and* has caused great harm for Your special people in Jerusalem. [14]I've heard that he has been authorized by the religious authorities to come here and chain everyone who associates with Your name.

Lord | [15]*None of that matters anymore!* Go! I have chosen him to be My instrument to bring My name far and wide—to Gentiles, to kings, and to the people of Israel as well. [16]I have much to show him, including how much he must suffer for My name.

[17]So Ananias went and entered the house *where Saul was staying.* He laid his hands on Saul and called to him.

Ananias | Brother Saul, the Lord Jesus, who appeared to you on your way here, sent me so you can regain your sight and be filled with the Holy Spirit.

[18]At that instant, something like scales fell from Saul's eyes, and he could see. So he got up, received the ceremonial washing* *identifying him as a disciple,* [19]ate some food *(remember, he had not eaten for three days),* and regained his strength. He spent a lot of time with the disciples in Damascus over the next several days—*as their brother, not their persecutor.* [20]Then he went into the very synagogues he had intended to purge, proclaiming,

Saul | Jesus is the Liberating King!

[21]Obviously this amazed everybody, and the buzz spread.

The People | Isn't he the man who caused so much trouble in Jerusalem for everyone identified with Jesus? Didn't he come here to arrest followers of Jesus and bring them in chains to the religious authorities? *Now he's switched sides and is preaching Jesus?*

[22]As time passed, Saul's confidence grew stronger and stronger, so much so that he debated with the Jews of Damascus and made an irrefutable case that Jesus is, in fact, the Messiah, the Liberating King.
[23]*They didn't like being confounded like this,* so, after several days, the Jews plotted to assassinate Saul. [24]But he learned of the plot. He knew they were keeping the city gates under constant surveillance, so they could follow and kill him when he left. [25]*To save Saul, the disciples came up*

9:18 Literally, immersion, a rite of initiation and purification *with a plan of their own.* They put Saul in a basket and lowered him by ropes from an opening in the wall of the city *so he never even passed through the gates. Their plan worked,* ²⁶and he returned to Jerusalem.

Things didn't go well for Saul in Jerusalem, though. He tried to join the disciples there, but they didn't think he was sincere.

²⁷*Only one person accepted Saul as a genuine disciple, and he was Barnabas, who, you remember, received this nickname because of his encouraging spirit.* Barnabas became Saul's advocate to the apostles. He told the whole story of what happened in Damascus, from Saul's vision and message from the Lord to his transformation into a confident proclaimer of the name of Jesus. ²⁸Finally, they accepted Saul and gave him access to their community, and he continued to speak confidently in the name of the Lord. ²⁹He dialogued—and argued—with a group of Greek-speaking Jews. *That didn't go well either, because soon* they were plotting to kill him also. ³⁰His fellow believers helped him escape by bringing him to Caesarea and sending him to *his hometown,* Tarsus.

³¹And so the church enjoyed a period of peace and growth throughout the regions of Judea, Galilee, and Samaria. The disciples lived in deep reverence for the Lord, they experienced the strong comfort of the Holy Spirit, and their numbers increased.

³²*Peter hadn't been idle during all this time.* He was having a number of amazing experiences of his own, traveling from group to group and visiting the various communities of believers. Once, he came to a town called Lydda, *a border town between Samaria and Judea,* and met with God's special people there. ³³He visited a man named Aeneas. This poor fellow had been paralyzed for eight years, unable to leave his bed.

Peter | ³⁴Aeneas, Jesus the Liberating King heals you. Get up! Now you can make your own bed!

And immediately—he got up! ³⁵*All the local residents*—both of Lydda and nearby Sharon—saw Aeneas *healthy and strong again,* so they turned to the Lord.

³⁶In a nearby *coastal* city, Joppa, there lived a disciple whose *Aramaic* name was Tabitha, or Dorcas in Greek. She was a good woman—devotedly doing good and giving to the poor. ³⁷While Peter was in Lydda, she fell sick and died. Her fellow disciples washed her body and laid her in an upstairs room. ³⁸They had heard Peter was nearby, so two of them went with an urgent message, "Please come to Joppa as soon as possible."

³⁹Peter went with them and immediately entered the room where the corpse had been placed. *It was quite a scene*—the widows *of the community* were crowded in the room, weeping, showing the various items of clothing that Dorcas had made for them.

⁴⁰Peter asked them to leave the room; then he got on his knees. He prayed *for a while* and then turned to her body.

Peter | Tabitha, get up!

She opened her eyes, saw Peter, and sat up. ⁴¹Giving her his hand, Peter lifted her up. Then he called in the other disciples—including the widows—and reintroduced them to their beloved friend. ⁴²The news of this miracle spread throughout the city, and many believed in the Lord. ⁴³Peter stayed in Joppa for some time as the guest of Simon, a tanner by profession.

GOD PLAYS NO FAVORITES

¹While Peter was in Joppa, another story was developing a day's journey to the north along the Mediterranean coast, in Caesarea. Cornelius, a Roman Centurion and a member of *a unit called* the Italian Cohort, lived there. *²Cornelius was a Gentile,* but he was a devout man—a God-fearing fellow with a God-fearing family. He consistently and generously gave to the poor, and he practiced constant prayer to God. ³About three o'clock one afternoon he had a vision of an angel of God. *Everything in the vision seemed so distinct, so real.*

Angel | Cornelius!

Cornelius | ⁴What is it, sir?
(terrified)

Angel | God has heard your prayers, and He has seen your kindness to the poor. *God has taken notice of you.* ⁵⁻⁶Send men *south* to Joppa, to the house of a tanner named Simon. Ask to speak to a guest of his named Simon, but also called Peter. You'll find this house near the waterfront.

⁷After the angel departed, Cornelius immediately called two of his slaves and a soldier under his command—an especially devout soldier. ⁸He told them the whole story and sent them to Joppa.

⁹Just as these men were nearing Joppa about noon the next day, Peter went up on the flat rooftop *of Simon the tanner's house.* He planned

to pray, [10]but he soon grew hungry. While his lunch was being prepared, Peter had a vision of his own—*a vision that linked his present hunger with what was about to happen:* [11]A rift opens in the sky and a wide container—something like a huge sheet suspended by its four corners—descends through the torn opening toward the ground. [12]This container teems with four-footed animals, creatures that crawl, and birds—*pigs, bats, lizards, snakes, frogs, toads, and vultures.*

A Voice | [13]Get up, Peter! Kill! Eat!

Peter | [14]No way, Lord! *These animals are disgusting! They're forbidden in the dietary laws of the Hebrew Scriptures!* I've never eaten non-kosher foods like these before—*not once in my life!*

A Voice | [15]If God calls something permissible and clean, you must not call it forbidden and dirty!

[16]Peter saw this vision three times, but the third time, the container of animals flew up through the rift in the sky, the rift healed, [17]and Peter was confused and unsettled as he tried to make sense of this strange vision.

At that very moment, *Peter heard the voices* of Cornelius's delegation, who had asked for directions to Simon's house, coming from the front gate.

Delegation | [18]Is there a man named Simon, also called Peter, staying at this house?

¹⁹⁻²⁰Peter's mind was still racing about the vision when the voice of the Holy Spirit broke through his churning thoughts.

> **Holy Spirit** | The three men who are searching for you have been sent by Me. So get up! Go with them. Don't hesitate or argue.

²¹Peter rushed downstairs to the men.

> **Peter** | I'm the one you're seeking. Can you tell me why you've come?

> **Delegation** | ²²We've been sent by *our commander and master*, Cornelius. He is a Centurion, and he is a *good, honest Gentile* who worships your God. All the Jewish people speak well of him. A holy angel told him to send for you so you would come to his home and he could hear your message.

³Peter extended hospitality to them and gave them lodging overnight. When they departed together the next morning, Peter brought some believers from Joppa.

²⁴They arrived in Caesarea the next afternoon *just before three o'clock.* Cornelius had anticipated their arrival and had assembled his relatives and close friends *to welcome them.* ²⁵When Peter and Cornelius met, Cornelius fell at Peter's feet in worship, ²⁶but Peter helped him up.

> **Peter** | Stand up, *man*! I am just a human being!

²⁷They talked and entered the house to meet the whole crowd inside.

Peter | ²⁸You know *I am a Jew. I would never enter the home of Gentiles like yourselves.* We Jews consider it a breach of divine law to associate, much less share hospitality, with Gentiles. But God has shown me something in recent days: I should no longer consider any human beneath me or unclean. ²⁹That's why I made no objection when you invited me; rather, I came willingly. Now, let me hear the story of why you invited me here.

Cornelius | ³⁰It was about this time of day four days ago when I was here, in my house, praying the customary mid-afternoon prayer. Suddenly, a man appeared out of nowhere. His clothes were dazzling white, and he stood directly in front of me ³¹and addressed me: "Cornelius, your prayer has been heard and your kindness to the poor has been noticed by God. ³²God wants you to find a man in Joppa, Simon who is also called Peter, who is staying at the home of a tanner named Simon, near the seaside." ³³I wasted no time, *did just as I was told,* and you have generously accepted my invitation. So here we are, in the presence of God, ready to take in all that the Lord has told you to tell us.

Peter | ³⁴It is clear to me now that God plays no favorites, ³⁵that God accepts every person whatever his or her culture or ethnic background, that God welcomes all who revere Him and do right. ³⁶*You already know that*

God sent a message to the people of Israel; it was a message of peace, peace through Jesus the Liberating King—who is King of all people. [37]You know this message spread through Judea, beginning in Galilee where John called people to be washed ceremonially.* [38]You know God identified Jesus as the uniquely chosen One by pouring out the Holy Spirit on Him, by empowering Him. You know Jesus went through the land doing good *for all* and healing all who were suffering under the oppression of the Evil One, for God was with Him. [39]My friends and I stand as witnesses to all Jesus did in the *region of* Judea and *the city of* Jerusalem. The people of our capital city killed Him by hanging Him on a tree, [40]but God raised Him up on the third day and made it possible for us to see Him. [41]Not everyone was granted this privilege, only those of us whom God chose as witnesses. We actually ate and drank with Him after His resurrection. [42]He told us to spread His message to everyone and to tell them that He is the One whom God has chosen to be Judge, *to make a just assessment of all people*—both living and dead. [43]All the prophets tell us about Him and assert that every person who believes in Jesus receives forgiveness of sins through His name.

*T*he true gospel was becoming increasingly clear as the church developed. Christianity is about being vulnerable. It is not about

---

10:37 Literally, immersed, in a rite of initiation and purification

elevating ourselves, but about having true humility rather than focusing on "me." Real Christianity looks to conquer and bridge divides, not habitually to separate.

What the law shows is that all have sinned. Many Jews were using it to show their superiority, but the new covenant had torn that system down before their eyes.

⁴⁴*Peter wasn't planning to stop at this point, but he could go no further because* the Holy Spirit suddenly interrupted and came upon all the people who were listening. ⁴⁵⁻⁴⁶They began speaking in foreign languages *(just as the Jewish disciples did on the Day of Pentecost),* and their hearts overflowed in joyful praises to God. Peter's friends *from Joppa*—all of them Jewish, all circumcised—were stunned to see that the gift of the Holy Spirit was poured out even on Gentiles.

> **Peter** | ⁴⁷Can anyone give any good reason not to ceremonially wash* these people *as fellow disciples? After all, it's obvious* they have received the Holy Spirit just as we did *on the Day of Pentecost.*

⁴⁸So, he had them washed ceremonially* in the name of Jesus the Liberating King. The new disciples asked him to stay for several more days.

10:47 Literally, immerse, in a rite of initiation and purification
10:48 Literally, immersed, in a rite of initiation and purification

No Argument, Only Silence

¹⁻²*By the time Peter and his friends from Joppa returned to Jerusalem,* news about Gentiles accepting God's message had already spread to the apostles and believers there. The circumcised believers didn't welcome Peter with joy, but with criticism.

Circumcised Believers	³*Why did you violate divine law by* associating with Gentiles and sitting at the table with them for a meal? *This is an outrage!*

⁴Peter patiently told them what had happened, laying out in detail the whole story.

Peter	⁵I was in Joppa, I was praying, and I fell into a trance. In my vision, something like a huge sheet descended from the sky as if it were being lowered by its four corners. It landed right in front of me. ⁶It was full of all kinds of creatures that we would call unclean—I could identify mammals, snakes, lizards, and birds. ⁷Then I heard a Voice say, "Get up, Peter! Kill these creatures and eat them!" ⁸*Of course,* I replied, "No way, Lord! Not a single bite of forbidden, non-kosher food has ever touched my lips." ⁹But then the Voice spoke from heaven a second time: "If God makes something clean, you must not call it dirty or forbidden." ¹⁰This

whole drama was repeated three times, and then it was all pulled back up into the sky.

¹¹At that very second, three men arrived at the house where I was staying. They had come to me from Caesarea. ¹²The Holy Spirit told me I should go with them, that I shouldn't make any distinction *between them as Gentiles and us as Jews*. These six brothers *from Joppa* came with me, and, yes, we entered the man's home, *even though he was a Gentile*.

¹³*The Gentile* told us the story of how he had seen an angel standing in his house who said, "Send to Joppa and bring back Simon, also called Peter, ¹⁴and he will give you a message that will rescue both you and your household." ¹⁵Then I began to speak, and as I did, the Holy Spirit fell upon them—it was exactly as it had been with us at the beginning. ¹⁶Then I remembered what Jesus had said to us: "John ritually cleansed* with water, but you will be cleansed with the Holy Spirit."* ¹⁷So, if God gave them the same gift we were given when we believed in the Lord Jesus, the Liberating King, who was I to stand in God's way?

¹⁸There was no argument, only silence.

Circumcised Believers | Well then, we must conclude that God has given to the Gentiles the opportunity to rethink their lives, turn to God, and gain a new life.

11:16 Literally, immersed, to show repentance
11:16 Acts 1:5

And so they stopped criticizing and started praising God.

[19]*Remember the persecution that began after Stephen's execution? The believers* who were scattered *from Judea* because of the persecution *following Stephen's stoning* kept moving out, reaching Phoenicia, Cyprus, and Antioch. Until this time, they had only shared their message with Jews. [20]Then, some men from Cyprus and Cyrene who had become believers came to Antioch, and they began sharing the message of the Lord Jesus with some Greek *converts to Judaism.* [21]The Lord was at work through them, and a large number *of these Greeks became* believers and turned to the Lord Jesus.

[22]Word of this new development came to the church in Jerusalem, and they sent Barnabas to Antioch *to investigate.* [23]He arrived and saw God's grace in action there, so he rejoiced and urged them to remain faithful to the Lord, to maintain an enduring, unshakable devotion. [24]*This Barnabas* truly was a good man, full of the Holy Spirit, full of faith. A very large number of people were brought to the Lord.

[25]*Barnabas soon was off again*—now to Tarsus to look for Saul. [26]He found Saul and brought him back to Antioch. The two of them spent an entire year there, meeting with the church, teaching huge numbers of people. It was there, in Antioch, where the term "Christian" was first used to identify disciples of Jesus.

[27]During that year, some prophets came north from Jerusalem to Antioch. [28]*A prophet named* Agabus stood in a meeting and made a prediction by the Holy Spirit: there would be an expansive, terrible famine in the whole region during the reign of Claudius. [29]*In anticipation of the famine,* the disciples determined to give an amount proportionate to their financial ability and create a relief fund for all the believers in Judea. [30]They sent Barnabas and Saul to carry this fund to the elders *in Jerusalem.*

Acts 12

PETER'S LAST NIGHT?

Back in Jerusalem, hard times came to the disciples. King Herod violently seized some who belonged to the church with the intention of mistreating them. [2]He ordered James (brother of John) to be executed by the sword, *the first apostle to be martyred.* [3]This move pleased Jewish public opinion, so he decided to arrest Peter also. During the holy festival of Unleavened Bread, [4]he caught Peter and imprisoned him, assigning four squads of soldiers to guard him. He planned to publicly *execute him* after the Passover holiday.

[5]During Peter's imprisonment, the church prayed constantly and intensely to God for his safety. [6]*Their prayers were not answered,* until the night before Peter's execution. *Picture this event:* Peter is sound asleep between two soldiers, double-chained, with still more guards outside the prison door watching for external intruders. [7]Suddenly, the cell fills with light: it is an angel of the Lord manifesting himself. He taps Peter on the side, awakening him.

Angel | Get up, quickly.

The chains fall off Peter's wrists.

Angel | [8]Come on! Put on your belt. Put on your sandals.

Peter puts them on *and just stands there.*

Angel | Pull your cloak over your shoulders. *Come on!* Follow me!

⁹Peter does so, but he is completely dazed. He doesn't think this is really happening—he assumes he is dreaming or having a vision. ¹⁰They pass the first guard. They pass the second guard. They come to the iron gate that opens to the city. The gate swings open for them on its own, and they walk into a lane. Suddenly, the angel disappears. ¹¹Peter finally realized all that had really happened.

Peter | *Amazing!* The Lord has sent His angel to rescue me from Herod and the public spectacle *of my execution.*

¹²Peter immediately rushed over to the home of a woman named Mary. (Mary's son, John Mark, *would eventually become an important associate of the apostles.*) A large group had gathered there to pray *for Peter and his safety.* ¹³He knocked at the outer gate, and a maid, Rhoda, answered. ¹⁴She recognized Peter's voice, but she was so overcome with excitement that she left him standing on the street and ran inside to tell everyone.

Rhoda | *Our prayers were answered!* Peter is at the front gate!

Praying Believers | ¹⁵*Rhoda, you're crazy!*

Rhoda | *No! Peter's out there! I'm sure of it!*

Praying Believers | Well, maybe it's his *guardian* angel *or something.*

¹⁶All this time, Peter was still out in the street, knocking on the gate. *Finally,* they came and let him in. *Of course, the disciples* were stunned, *and everyone was talking at once.* ¹⁷Peter motioned for them to quiet down and then told them the amazing story of how the Lord engineered his escape.

*O*n the night before his execution, Peter slept like a baby. Here he was, chained in a room full of soldiers, James's blood still moist on the ground, and though he could only assume this was his one last night before his own torturous death, he was not afraid. So peacefully did he rest, in fact, that the angel had to prod him to wake up, and even while he was walking, he questioned if he was dreaming. Meanwhile, the believers had dropped everything and gathered together to pray. Was this the thought that kept Peter at peace? That his friends and family were on their knees all day appealing to God for him? Maybe. But certainly Peter trusted that God was in control. A church that started with 12 people was now over 8,000, and God was blessing the world through these people.

Peter | Could you please get word to James and the other believers *that I'm all right?*

Then he left to find a safer place to stay.

[18]*Meanwhile, the soldiers were having a good night's sleep.* But when morning came and Peter was gone, there was a huge uproar among the soldiers. [19]Herod *sent troops* to find Peter, but he was missing. Herod interrogated the guards and ordered their executions. Peter headed down toward the coast to Caesarea, and he remained there.

[20]*King Herod had other problems at this time. There was a major political upheaval to deal with.* Herod was at odds with the populace of neighboring Tyre and Sidon, so the two cities sent a large group of representatives to meet with him. They won over one of Herod's closest associ-

ates, Blastus, the director of the treasury; then they pressured Herod to drop his grudge. Cooperation was important to the two cities *because they were all major trading partners* and depended on Herod's territory for food. [21]*They struck a deal, and Herod came over to ratify it.* Dressed in all his royal finery and seated high above them on a platform, he made a speech, [22]and the people of Tyre and Sidon interrupted with cheers to flatter him.

The People | This is the voice of a god! This is no mere mortal!

[23]Herod should have given glory to the true God, *but since he vainly accepted their flattery,* that very day an angel of the Lord struck him with an illness. It was an ugly disease, involving putrefaction and worms eating his flesh. Eventually he died.

[24]Through all this upheaval, God's message spread to new frontiers and attracted more and more people. [25]Meanwhile, the time Barnabas and Saul *spent in Antioch came to an end,* and they reported back to Jerusalem, bringing along John, who was also called Mark. *After delivering the relief fund they had brought with them, the three men returned to Antioch.*

Acts 13

THE DUST OFF THEIR FEET

¹The church in Antioch *had grown strong*, with many prophets and teachers: Barnabas, Simeon (a dark man *from Central Africa*), Lucius (from Cyrene *in North Africa*), Manaen (a member of Herod's governing council), and Saul. ²Once they were engaged in a time of worship and fasting when the Holy Spirit spoke to them, "Commission Barnabas and Saul to a project I have called them to accomplish." ³They fasted and prayed some more, laid their hands on the two selected men, and sent them off on their new mission. ⁴Having received special commissioning by the Holy Spirit, Barnabas and Saul went to nearby Seleucia, *on the coast*. Then they caught a ship to the island of Cyprus.

⁵At the city of Salamis, *on the east side of Cyprus*, they proclaimed the message of God in Jewish synagogues, assisted by John Mark. ⁶⁻⁷*They went westward from town to town,* finally reaching Paphos on the western shore. There the proconsul, Sergius Paulus, an intelligent man, summoned Barnabas and Saul because he wanted to hear their message. At his side was an occult spiritualist and Jewish false prophet named Bar-Jesus or Elymas (which means "magician"). ⁸Elymas argued with Barnabas and Saul, trying to keep Sergius Paulus from coming to faith.

⁹Saul, now known as Paul, was suddenly full of the Holy Spirit. He stared directly into *Elymas's* face.

Paul | ¹⁰You're a son of the devil. You're an enemy of justice, and you're full of lies, and you steal opportunities from others. Why do you insist on confusing and twisting the clear, straight paths of the Lord? ¹¹Hear

this, *Elymas*: the Lord's hand is against you, and you
will be *as* blind *as a bat* for a period of time, *beginning
right now!*

At that instant, it was as if a mist came over Elymas, and then total
darkness. He stumbled around, groping for a hand *so he could be led back
home.* [12]When Sergius Paulus saw this happen, he came to faith and was
attracted to and amazed by the teaching about the Lord.

[13]Paul and his entourage *boarded a ship* and set sail from Paphos.
They traveled *north* to Perga in Pamphylia. John Mark, however, abandoned the mission and returned to Jerusalem.

[14]Paul and Barnabas continued from Perga to Pisidian Antioch, and
on the Sabbath, they entered the synagogue and sat down. [15]After the
regular reading of the Hebrew Scriptures—including passages from
the Law and the Prophets—the synagogue leaders sent a message to
them: "Brothers, if you would like to give us some exhortation, please
do so." [16]Paul rose to his feet, offered a gesture of greeting, and began
his message.

Paul | Israelites and other God-fearing people, please hear
me. [17]The God of the Israelites chose our ancestors
and helped them become a large population while
they were living in Egypt many years ago. He dis-
played His great power by leading them out *of that
powerful nation.* [18]For about 40 years, He endured their
constant complaining in the wilderness. [19]He opened
up some land for them in Canaan by destroying the
seven nations living there, and that land became their
inheritance for about 450 years. [20]They had tribal

leaders through the time of the prophet Samuel.
²¹Then they asked for a king, and God gave them
one—Saul, son of Kish, of the tribe of Benjamin—who
reigned for 40 years. ²²God moved Saul aside and made
David king instead. God had this to say about David: "I
have found David, son of Jesse, to be a man after My
own heart. He's the kind of king who will rule in ways
that please Me."* ²³God has selected one of David's
descendants as the long-promised Liberator of Israel. I
am speaking of Jesus.

²⁴*Before Jesus arrived on the scene,* His *cousin* John *was
hard at work,* proclaiming to all the people of Israel a
ritual cleansing* pointing to a new direction in
thought and life. ²⁵John's ministry climaxed when he
said, "Who do you assume me to be? I am not the One
you're looking for. No, but One is coming after me, One
whose sandal thong I am unworthy to untie."* ²⁶My
brothers, fellow descendants of our common father
Abraham, and others here who fear God, we are the
ones to whom God has sent this message of salvation.

²⁷But you know the people of Jerusalem and their
leaders did not recognize Jesus. They didn't understand the words of the prophets that are read *in the
synagogues on* Sabbath after Sabbath. As a result, they
fulfilled the ancient prophecies by condemning Jesus.
²⁸Even though they could find no offense punishable
by death, still they asked Pilate to execute Jesus.

13:22 1 Samuel 13:14
13:24 Literally, immersion, an act of show repentance
13:25 Luke 3:16

²⁹When they carried out everything that had been foretold by the prophets, they took His body down from the tree and laid Him in a tomb. ³⁰But *that was not the end:* God raised Him from the dead, ³¹and over a period of many days He appeared to those who had been His companions from *the beginning of their journey in* Galilee until *its end in* Jerusalem. They are now witnesses to everyone. ³²We are here to bring you the good news of God's promise to our ancestors, ³³which He has now fulfilled for our children by raising Jesus. *Consider the promises fulfilled in Jesus.* The psalmist says, "You are My Son; today I have become Your Father."*

³⁴Elsewhere God promises that Jesus will rise and never return to death and corruption again: "I will make You the holy and faithful promises I made to David."* ³⁵Similarly, another psalm says, "You will not abandon Me to experience suffering of a miserable afterlife. Nor leave Me to rot alone. "* ³⁶*We all know* David died and was reduced to dust after he served God's purpose in his generation; ³⁷these words *obviously* apply *not to David but* to the One God raised from death before suffering decay. ³⁸So you must realize, my brothers, that through *this resurrected Man* forgiveness of sins is assured to you. ³⁹Through *Jesus*, everyone who believes is set free from all sins—sins which the law of Moses could not release you from. ⁴⁰In light of all this, be careful that you do not fulfill these words

---

13:33 Psalm 2:7
13:34 Isaiah 55:3
13:35 Psalm 16:10

of the prophet *Habakkuk*: [41]"Look, you who live among the Gentiles! Be shocked to death, for in your days I am doing a work, a work you will never believe, even if someone tells you plainly!"*

[42]Paul and Barnabas prepared to leave *the synagogue*, but the people wanted to hear more and urged them to return the following Sabbath. [43]As the people dispersed after the meeting, many Jews and converts to Judaism followed Paul and Barnabas. *Privately,* Paul and Barnabas continued teaching them and urged them to remain steadfast in the grace of God. [44]The next Sabbath, it seemed the whole city had gathered to hear the message of the Lord. [45]But some of the Jewish leaders were jealous when they saw these huge crowds. They began to *argue with and* contradict Paul's message, as well as slander him. [46]Paul and Barnabas together responded with great confidence.

Paul and Barnabas | *OK, then.* It was only right that we should bring God's message to you *Jewish people* first. But now, since you are rejecting our message and identifying yourselves as unworthy of eternal life, we are turning to the Gentiles. [47]The Lord has commanded us to do this. *Remember His words:* "He is a light to the nations beyond Israel, and He is the liberation of Your covenant people, Israel. "*

[48]*These words created two strong reactions.* The Gentiles were thrilled and praised God's message, and all those who had been appointed for eter-

---

13:41 Habakkuk 1:5
13:47 Isaiah 49:6

nal life became believers. [49]*Through them* the Lord's message spread through the whole region *of Cyprus*. [50]But the Jewish leaders united the aristocratic religious women and the city's leading men in opposition to Paul and Barnabas, and soon they were persecuted and driven out of *Cyprus*. [51]They simply shook the dust off their feet in protest and moved on to Iconium. [52]The disciples *weren't intimidated at all; rather,* they were full of joy and the Holy Spirit.

Acts 14

ON YOUR OWN TWO FEET, MAN

¹*The results* in Iconium *were similar*. Paul and Barnabas began in the Jewish synagogue, bringing a great number of ethnic Jews and Greek converts to faith in Jesus. ²But the other Jews who wouldn't believe agitated the Gentiles and poisoned their minds against the brothers. ³Paul and Barnabas stayed in Iconium for a long time, speaking with great confidence for the Lord. He confirmed the message of His grace by granting them the power to do signs and wonders. ⁴But *over time* the people were divided, some siding with the *unbelieving* Jews and some siding with the apostles. ⁵*Finally,* the Jews and Gentiles who opposed the apostles joined forces and enlisted the political leaders in their plan to beat and stone Paul and Barnabas. ⁶The apostles learned of the plan and escaped to Lystra and Derbe in Lycaonia, and the surrounding countryside, ⁷where they continued proclaiming the good news.

⁸In Lystra, they met a man who had been crippled since birth; his feet were completely useless. ⁹He listened to Paul speak, and Paul could see in this man's face that he had faith to be healed.

Paul
(shouting) | ¹⁰Stand up on your own two feet, *man*!

The man jumped up and walked! ¹¹When the crowds saw this, they started shouting in Lycaonian.

Crowd | The gods have come down to us! They've come in human form!

[12]They decided that Barnabas was Zeus and Paul was Hermes (since he was the main speaker). [13]*Before they knew it,* the priest of Zeus, whose temple was prominent in that city, came to the city gates with oxen and garlands of flowers so the Lycaonians could offer sacrifices in worship *to Paul and Barnabas!* [14]When they heard of this, Paul and Barnabas were beside themselves with frustration—they ripped their tunics *as an expression of disapproval* and rushed out into the crowd.

Paul and Barnabas
(shouting)

[15]Friends! No! No! Don't do this! We're just humans like all of you! *We're not here to be worshiped!*
We're here to bring you good news, good news that you should turn from these worthless forms of worship and instead serve the living God, the God who made the heaven and the earth and the sea and all that they contain. [16]Through all previous generations God has allowed all the nations to follow their own customs and religions, [17]but even then God revealed Himself by doing good to you—giving you rain for your crops and fruitful harvests season after season, filling your stomachs with food and your hearts with joy.

[18]In spite of these words, they were barely able to keep the crowds from making sacrifices to them.

*W*e struggle to keep the focus on the one true God. When God uses men to bless the world, many mistakenly exalt those men to the place of God. This inevitably leads to pain and disappointment. Paul and Barnabas did the right thing by shouting as loudly as possible, "We are only men!" It is time for many leaders and celebrities to follow their example, root out the religious hero worship, claim our humanity, and start sharing our own struggles—sin, depression, despair—to remind people we are all alike.

[19]Then *unbelieving* Jews came from Antioch and Iconium and *incited the crowds against the apostles.* The crowds turned on Paul, stoned him, dragged him out of the city, and left him there, thinking he was dead. [20]As the disciples gathered around him, he suddenly rose to his feet and returned to the city. The next day he and Barnabas left for Derbe. [21]After they proclaimed the good news there and taught many disciples, they returned to *some of the cities they had recently visited*—Lystra, Iconium, and Antioch *in Pisidia.* [22]In each place they brought strength to the disciples, encouraging them to remain true to the faith.

Paul and Barnabas | We must go through many persecutions as we enter the kingdom of God.

[23]In each church they would appoint leaders, pray and fast together, and entrust them to the Lord in whom they had come to believe.

[24]They then passed through Pisidia and came to Pamphylia. [25]They preached their message in Perga and then went to the port of Attalia. [26]There they set sail for Antioch, where they were first entrusted to the grace of God for the mission they had now completed. [27]They called the church together when they arrived and reported all God had done with *and through them,* how God had welcomed Gentiles through the doorway of faith. [28]They stayed with the disciples *in Antioch* for quite a while.

NOT BURDEN THE GENTILES

¹*Their peace was disturbed, however,* when certain Judeans came with this teaching: "Unless you are circumcised according to Mosaic custom, you cannot be saved." ²Paul and Barnabas argued against this teaching and debated with the Judeans vehemently, so the church selected several people—including Paul and Barnabas—to travel to Jerusalem to dialogue about this issue with the apostles and elders there. ³The church sent them on their way. They passed through Phoenicia and Samaria, stopping to report to the groups of believers there that Gentiles were now being converted. This brought great joy to them all. ⁴Upon arrival in Jerusalem, the church, the apostles, and the elders welcomed them warmly, and they reported all they had seen God do. ⁵But there were some believers present who belonged to the sect of the Pharisees. They stood up and asserted,

> **Pharisees** | No, this is not acceptable. These people must be circumcised, and we must require them to keep the whole Mosaic Law.

⁶The apostles and elders met privately to discuss how this issue should be resolved. ⁷There was a lot of debate, and finally Peter stood up.

> **Peter** | My brothers, you all know that in the early days *of our movement* God decided that I should be the one through whom the first Gentiles would hear the good news and become believers. ⁸God knows the human

heart, and He showed approval of their hearts by giving them the Holy Spirit just as He did for us. [9]In cleansing their hearts by faith, God has made no distinction between them and us. [10]So it makes no sense to me that some of you are testing God by burdening His disciples with a load that neither our forefathers nor we have been able to carry. [11]No, we *all* believe that we will be liberated through the grace of the Lord Jesus—they also will be rescued in the same way.

[12]There was silence among them while Barnabas and Paul reported all the miraculous signs and wonders God had done through them among Gentiles. [13]When they finished, James spoke.

James | My brothers, hear me. [14]Simon *Peter* reminded us how God first included Gentiles in His favor, taking people from among the Gentiles for His name. [15]This resonates with the words of the prophets: [16]"After this, [I will return] and rebuild the house of David, which has fallen into ruins. From its wreckage I will rebuild it, [17]so all the nations may seek the Lord—including every person among the Gentile nations who has been called by My name."* [18]This is the word of the Lord, who has been revealing these things since ancient times.

[19]So here is my counsel: we should not burden these Gentiles who are turning to God. [20]We should instead write a letter, instructing them to abstain

15:17 Amos 9:11-12

from *four* things: first, things associated with idol worship; second, sexual immorality; third, food killed by strangling; and fourth, blood. [21]*My reason for these four exceptions* is that in every city there are Jewish communities where, for generations, the laws of Moses have been proclaimed, and on every Sabbath Moses is read in synagogues everywhere.

[22]This seemed like a good idea to the apostles, the elders, and the entire church. They commissioned men from among them and sent them to Antioch with Paul and Barnabas. They sent two prominent men among the believers, Judas (also known as Barsabbas) and Silas, [23]to deliver this letter:

> The brotherhood, including the apostles and elders in Jerusalem, send greetings to the Gentile believers in Antioch, Syria, and Cilicia. [24]We have heard that certain people from among us—without authorization from us—have said things that, in turn, upset you and unsettle your minds. [25]We have decided unanimously to choose and send *two* representatives, along with our beloved Barnabas and Paul, [26]who, *as you know,* have risked their lives for our Lord Jesus the Liberating King. [27]These representatives, Judas and Silas, will confirm verbally what you will read in this letter. [28]It has seemed good to the Holy Spirit and to us to keep you free from all burdens except these four: [29]abstain from anything sacrificed to idols, from blood, from food killed by strangling, and from sexual immorality. Avoid these things, and you will be just fine. Farewell.

[30]So the men were sent to Antioch. When they arrived, they gathered the community together and read the letter. [31]The community

rejoiced at the resolution to the controversy. ³²Judas and Silas, being prophets themselves, offered lengthy encouragements to strengthen the believers. ³³After some time there, they returned in peace to *the Jerusalem community.* ³⁴[After some thought, Silas decided to remain behind.*] ³⁵Paul and Barnabas stayed in Antioch, where they teamed with many others to teach and preach the message of the Lord.

³⁶Some days later, Paul *proposed another journey* to Barnabas.

> **Paul** | Let's return and visit the believers in each city where we preached the Lord's message *last time* to see how they're doing.

³⁷Barnabas agreed and wanted to bring John Mark along, ³⁸but Paul felt that was a mistake since John Mark had abandoned them in Pamphylia and hadn't finished the previous mission. ³⁹Their difference of opinion was so heated that they decided not to work together anymore. Barnabas took John Mark and sailed to Cyprus, ⁴⁰while Paul chose Silas *as his companion.* The believers *in Antioch* commissioned him for this work, entrusting him to the grace of the Lord. ⁴¹They traveled through Syria and Cilicia to strengthen the churches there.

15:34 This verse is omitted from the earliest manuscripts.

TIMOTHY OF GOOD REPUTATION

¹⁻³When Paul reached Derbe and Lystra, he invited a disciple named Timothy to join him *and Silas*. Timothy had a good reputation among the believers in Lystra and Iconium, *but there was a problem*: although Timothy's mother was a believing Jew, his father was Greek, *which meant Timothy was uncircumcised*. Because the Jewish people of those cities knew he was the son of a Greek man, Paul felt it would be best for Timothy to be circumcised before proceeding.

⁴Leaving there, *now accompanied by Timothy*, they delivered to the churches in each town the decisions and instructions given by the apostles and elders in Jerusalem. ⁵The churches were strengthened in the faith by their visit and kept growing in numbers on a daily basis.

⁶They sensed the Holy Spirit telling them not to preach their message in Asia at this time, so they traveled through Phrygia and Galatia. ⁷They came near Mysia and planned to go into Bithynia, but again, they felt restrained from doing so by the Spirit of Jesus. ⁸So they bypassed Mysia and went down to Troas. ⁹That night, Paul had a vision in which a Macedonian man was pleading with him.

Macedonian Man | Come over to Macedonia! Come help us!

¹⁰This vision convinced us all—*I should add that I, Luke, had joined Paul, Silas, and Timothy by this time*—that God was calling us to bring the good news to that region.

¹¹We set sail from the port city of Troas, first stopping in Samothrace, then the next day in Neapolis, ¹²finally arriving in Philippi,

a Roman colony and one of Macedonia's leading cities. We stayed in Philippi for several days. ¹³On the Sabbath day, we went outside the city walls to the nearby river, assuming that *some Jewish people* might be gathering for prayer. We found a group of women there, so we sat down and spoke to them. ¹⁴One of them, Lydia, was *a business woman* originally from Thyatira. She made a living buying and selling fine purple fabric. She was a true worshiper of God and listened to Paul *with special interest*. The Lord opened her heart to take in the message with enthusiasm. ¹⁵She and her whole household were ceremonially washed.*

> **Lydia** | If you believe I'm truly faithful to the Lord, please, you must come and stay at my home.

We couldn't turn down her invitation.

¹⁶One day, as we were going to the place set aside for prayer, we encountered a slave girl. She made a lot of money for her owners as a fortune-teller, assisted by some sort of occult spirit. ¹⁷She began following us.

> **Slave Girl** | These men are slaves like me, but slaves of the Most
> *(shouting)* | High God! They will proclaim to you the way of
> liberation!

¹⁸The next day as we passed by, she did the same thing—and again on the following days. One day Paul was really annoyed, so he turned and spoke to the spirit that was enslaving her.

> **Paul** | I order you in the name of Jesus the Liberating King: Come out of her!

16:15 Literally, immersed, in a rite of initiation and purification

It came right out. [19]But when her owners realized she would be worth-less now as a fortune-teller, they grabbed Paul and Silas, dragged them into the open market area, and presented them to the authorities.

Slave Owners | [20]These men are troublemakers, disturbing the peace of our great city. They are from some Jewish sect, [21]and they promote foreign customs that violate our Roman standards of conduct.

[22]The crowd joined in with insults and insinuations, prompting the city officials to strip them naked in the public square so they could be beaten with rods. [23]They were flogged mercilessly and then were thrown into a prison cell. The jailer was ordered to keep them under the strictest supervision. [24]The jailer complied, first restraining them in ankle chains, then locking them in the most secure cell in the center of the jail.

[25]*Picture this:* It's midnight. *In the darkness of their cell,* Paul and Silas— *after surviving the severe beating*—aren't moaning and groaning; they're pray-ing and singing hymns to God. The prisoners *in adjoining cells are wide awake,* listening to them pray and sing. [26]Suddenly, the ground begins to shake, and the prison foundations begin to crack. *You can hear* the sound of jangling chains and the squeak of cell doors opening. Every prisoner realizes that his chains have come unfastened. [27]The jailer wakes up and runs into the jail. His heart sinks as he sees the doors have all swung open. He is sure his prisoners have escaped, and he knows this will mean death for him. So he decides to do the deed him-self and pulls out his sword to commit suicide. [28]At that moment, Paul sees what is happening and shouts out at the top of his lungs,

Paul | *Wait, man!* Don't harm yourself! We're all here! *None of us has escaped.*

²⁹The jailer sends his assistants to get some torches and rushes into the cell of Paul and Silas. He falls on his knees before them, trembling. ³⁰Then he brings them outside.

Jailer | Gentlemen, please tell me, what must I do to be liberated?

Paul and Silas | ³¹Just believe—believe in the ultimate King, Jesus, and not only will you be rescued, but your whole household will as well.

³²⁻³⁴The jailer brings them to his home, and they have a long conversation with the man and his family. Paul and Silas explain the message of Jesus to them all. The man washes their wounds and *feeds them*, then they ceremonially wash* the man and his family. The night ends with Paul and Silas in the jailer's home, sharing a meal together, the whole family rejoicing that they have come to faith in God.

³⁵At dawn, the city officials send the police *to the jailer's home* with a command: "Let those men go free."

Jailer | ³⁶The city officials have ordered me to release you, so you may go now, in peace.

Paul
(loud enough that the police can hear) | ³⁷Just a minute. This is unjust. We've been *stripped naked*, beaten in public, and thrown into jail, all without a trial of any kind. Now they want to secretly release us as if nothing happened? No way: we're Roman citizens—*we shouldn't be treated like this!* If the

---

16:32-34 Literally, immerse, in a rite of initiation and purification

city officials want to release us, then they can come
and tell us to our faces.

[38]The police report back to the city officials, and when they come to
the part about Paul and Silas being Roman citizens, the officials turn
pale with fear. [39]They rush to the jail in person and apologize. They
personally escort Paul and Silas from their cell and politely ask them to
leave the city. [40]Paul and Silas oblige—after stopping at Lydia's home to
gather with the brothers and sisters there and give them parting
words of encouragement.

*P*aul and Silas planned to keep a low profile because it was
clear that preaching the gospel openly was not going to advance the
cause of Christ. But in the course of their travels, Paul got annoyed. He
was tired of the recurring mantra of this evil spirit living in a slave girl.
He was not moved by sympathy or compassion for the girl. She was
simply getting on his nerves. So Paul performed his first miracle in the
area by casting out this evil spirit, which set off a totally unexpected
chain of events bringing them into the city court to be beaten before
the crowds. This would seem to be the start of a very bad day. I can
only imagine Silas saying, "Paul, what were you doing? Is your aggrava-
tion with this wandering girl worth all this trouble?" But they neither
fought nor despaired; instead, they sang, prayed to God, and loved their
captors. Paul and Silas demonstrated that we are not easily distracted
or depressed as long as serving God is our priority.

FAST TALKER

¹After leaving Philippi and passing through Amphipolis and Apollonia, Paul and Silas came to Thessalonica. There was a Jewish synagogue there. ²⁻³As he had done in other cities, Paul attended the synagogue and presented arguments, based on the Hebrew Scriptures, that the Liberating King had to suffer and rise from the dead.

> **Paul** | Who is this suffering and rising Liberator I am proclaiming to you? He is Jesus.

N He came back the next two Sabbaths—repeating the same pattern. ⁴Some of the *ethnically Jewish people from the synagogue* were persuaded and joined Paul and Silas. Even more devout Greeks *who had affiliated with Judaism* came to believe—along with quite a few of the city's leading women. ⁵⁻⁶*Seeing this movement growing*, the unconvinced Jewish people became protective and angry. They found some ruffians hanging out in the marketplaces and convinced them to help start a riot. Soon a mob formed, *and the whole city was seething with tension. The mob was going street by street*, looking for Paul and Silas—who were nowhere to be found. Frustrated, when the mob came to the house of a man named Jason, *now known as a believer*, they grabbed him and some other believers they found there and dragged them to the city officials.

> **Mob** | These people—they're *political agitators* turning the
> world upside down! They're stirring up rebellion
> everywhere; they've come here to our fine city, ⁷and

this man, Jason, has given them sanctuary *and made his house a base for their operations. We want to expose their real intent:* they are trying to overturn the entire empire! They're saying that Jesus is king, *not Caesar!*

[8]Of course, this disturbed the crowd at large and the city officials especially, [9]so they demanded bail from Jason and the others before releasing them.

[10]The believers waited until dark and then sent Paul and Silas off to Berea. When they arrived, they *repeated their usual pattern by* going to the synagogue *to proclaim Jesus from the Hebrew Scriptures.* [11]The Jewish people here were more receptive than they had been in Thessalonica. They warmly and enthusiastically welcomed the message and then, day by day, would check for themselves to see if what they heard from Paul and Silas was truly in harmony with the Hebrew Scriptures. [12]Many of them were convinced, and the new believers included—*as in Thessalonica*—quite a few of the city's leading Greek women, and important men also. [13]Reports got back to Thessalonica that Paul and Silas were now spreading God's message in Berea; the Jewish people who had incited the riot in Thessalonica quickly came to Berea to do the same once again. [14-15]The believers sent Paul away. A small group escorted him, first to the coast, and then all the way to Athens. Silas and Timothy, however, remained in Berea. Later, they received instructions from Paul to join him in Athens as soon as possible.

[16]So Paul found himself alone for some time in Athens. He would walk through the city, feeling deeply frustrated about the abundance of idols there. [17]*As in the previous cities*, he went to the synagogue. Once again, he engaged in debate *about Jesus* with both ethnic Jews and *devout Greek-born converts to Judaism. But this time, he didn't limit himself to*

the synagogue. He would even wander around in the marketplace, speaking with anyone he happened to meet. [18]Eventually, he got into a debate with some Epicurean and Stoic philosophers. Some were dismissive from the start.

Philosophers | What's this fast-talker trying to pitch?

Others | He seems to be advocating the gods of distant lands.

[19-21]This stirred their curiosity, because the favorite pastime of Athenians (including foreigners who had settled there) was conversation about new and unusual ideas. So they brought him to the rock outcropping known as the Areopagus, *where Athens' intellectuals regularly gathered for debate*, and they invited him to speak.

Athenians | May we understand this new teaching of yours? It is intriguingly unusual. We would love to understand its meaning.

Paul | [22]Athenians, *I am a new visitor to your beautiful city. As I have walked your streets*, I have observed your strong and diverse religious ethos. You truly are a religious people. [23]I have stopped again and again to examine carefully the religious statues and inscriptions that fill your city. In one such temple, I read this inscription: "TO AN UNKNOWN GOD." I am not here to tell you about a strange foreign deity, but about this One whom you already worship, though without full knowledge. [24]This is the God who made the universe and all it contains, the God who is *the Caesar*, the King, of all heaven and all earth. It would be illogical to assume that a God of this magnitude could possibly be contained in any man-made structure, no matter how majestic. *[25]Nor would it be logical to think that* this God would need human beings to provide Him with food and shelter—after all, He Himself would have given to humans everything they need—life, breath, *food, shelter, and so on. [26]This is the only universal God, the One who made all of us, wherever we now live, whatever our nationality or culture or religion.* This God made us in all our diversity from one original person, allowing each culture to have its own time to develop, giving each its own place to live and thrive in its distinct ways. *[27]His purpose in all this was* that people of every culture and religion would search for this ultimate God, grope for Him *in the darkness, as it were,* hoping to find Him. Yet, in truth, God is not far from any of us. [28]One of your own poets said, "We live in God; we move in God; we exist in God." And another said, "We are indeed God's children." [29]Since this is true, since we are indeed offspring of God's creative act, we shouldn't think of the Deity as our own artifact, something made by our own hands—as if this great, universal, ultimate Creator were simply a combination of elements like gold, silver, and stone. [30]No, God has patiently tolerated this kind of ignorance in the past, but now God says it is time to rethink our lives *and reject these unenlightened assumptions.* [31]He has fixed a day of accountability, when the whole world—including every culture and religion—will be justly evaluated by a new, higher standard: *not by a statue*, but by a living Man. God selected this Man and made Him credible to all by raising Him from the dead.

[32]When they heard that last phrase about resurrection from the dead, some shook their heads and scoffed, but others were even more curious.

Others | We would like you to come and speak to us again.

[33]Paul left at that point, [34]but some people followed him and came to faith, including one from Areopagus named Dionysius, a *prominent* woman named Damaris, and others.

*T*his exchange is the most potent example of cross-cultural evangelism in the Bible. Notice how Paul provokes his audience to think and invites them to pursue God, but he does not attempt to summarize the gospel in simple propositions or acronyms. He connects their culture with the truth of the gospel and the beauty of the person who is Jesus. After that, it's the job of the Holy Spirit. How can we follow this example?

THE DUST OFF HIS GARMENTS

¹From Athens, Paul traveled to Corinth *alone*. ²He found a Jewish man there named Aquila, originally from Pontus. Aquila and his wife Priscilla had recently come to Corinth from Italy because Claudius had banished all Jews from Rome. Paul visited them *in their home* ³and discovered they shared the same trade of tent making. He then became their long-term guest and joined them in their tentmaking business. ⁴Each Sabbath he would engage both Jews and Greeks in debate in the synagogue in an attempt to persuade them of his message. ⁵Eventually, Silas and Timothy left Macedonia and joined him in Corinth. They found him fully occupied by proclaiming the message, testifying to the Jewish people that their Liberator was Jesus. ⁶Eventually, though, some of them stopped listening and began insulting him. He shook the dust off his garments in protest.

> **Paul** | OK. I've done all I can for you. You are responsible for your own destiny before God. From now on, I will bring the good news to the Gentiles!

⁷He walked out of the synagogue and went next door to the home of *a Gentile*, Titius Justus, who worshiped God. ⁸*Paul formed a gathering of believers there that included* Crispus (the synagogue leader) and his whole household and many other Corinthians, who heard Paul, believed, and were baptized. ⁹One night Paul had a vision in which he heard the Lord's voice.

The Lord | Do not be afraid, Paul. Speak! Don't be silent! [10]I am with you and no one will lay a finger on you to harm you. I have many in this city who are already My people.

[11]*After such turmoil in previous cities*, these words encouraged Paul to extend his stay in Corinth, teaching the message of God among them for a year and six months.

*H*ave you ever been frustrated by arguments and bickering with your religious friends? Maybe your frustration is a sign that you are devoting your energies in the wrong places. Like Paul, your frustration could be God pushing you into new areas or new ministries. This man kept a smile on his face when he was stripped, beaten, and imprisoned, but religious bickering brought him to his wits' end. There is nothing more depressing than religious systems corrupted by arrogance and legalism. On the other hand, the greatest joys in life may be found when we passionately pursue the dangerous mission of the Liberating King.

[12]During this time, the Jews organized an attack on Paul and made formal charges against him to Gallio, the proconsul of Achaia.

Jews | [13]This man is convincing people to worship God in ways that contradict our Hebrew Scriptures.

Gallio | [14]Look, if this were some serious crime, I would accept your complaint as a legitimate legal case, [15]but this is just more of your typical Jewish squabbling about trivialities in your sacred literature. I have no interest in getting dragged into this kind of thing.

[16]*So he threw out their case and* drove them away from his bench. [17]They were furious and seized Sosthenes, the synagogue official; then they beat him in front of the tribunal. Gallio just ignored them.

[18]At the end of eighteen months, Paul said good-bye to the believers in Corinth. He wanted to travel *to the east and south* to Syria by ship, so, accompanied by Priscilla and Aquila, he went to the nearby port city of Cenchrea, where he fulfilled a vow he had made by cutting his hair. [19]The three of them sailed east to Ephesus where Paul would leave Priscilla and Aquila. Paul again went to the synagogue where he dialogued with the Jews. [20]They were receptive and invited him to stay longer.

Paul | [21-22]If God wills, I'll return at some point.

He caught a ship bound *south and east* for Caesarea by the sea. There he went up for a brief visit with the believers in the churches; then he headed north to Antioch. [23]He spent considerable time there and then left again, visiting city after city throughout Galatia and Phrygia, strengthening the disciples in each place.

[24]Meanwhile, back in Ephesus, a Jew named Apollos *made contact with the community of believers.* He had been raised in Alexandria, *Egypt, a place where Jewish intellectuals were seeking to integrate Greek philosophy with Judaism.* Apollos was eloquent and well educated in the Hebrew Scriptures. [25]He was partially instructed in the way of the Lord, and he added to his native eloquence a burning enthusiasm to teach about

Jesus. He taught accurately what he knew, *but he had only understood part of the good news*, specifically the ritual cleansing* preached by John, the forerunner of Jesus. ²⁶So, when Priscilla and Aquila heard him speak boldly in the synagogue, *they discerned both his gift and his lack of full understanding*. They took him aside and in private explained the way of God to him more accurately and fully. ²⁷He wanted to head west into Achaia, *where Paul had recently been*, to preach there. The believers encouraged him to do so and sent a letter instructing the *Greek* disciples to welcome him. Upon his arrival, he was of great help to all in Achaia who had, by the grace of God, become believers. ²⁸This gifted speaker publicly demonstrated, based on the Hebrew Scriptures, that the promised Liberating King is Jesus. Then, when the Jews there raised counterarguments, he refuted them with great power.

18:25 Literally, immersion, an act of repentance

AN INCOMPLETE GOSPEL

[1,7]While Apollos was in Corinth, Paul's overland journey brought him back to Ephesus. He encountered a group of about a dozen disciples there.

> **Paul** | [2]Did you receive the Holy Spirit when you became believers?

> **John's Disciples** | We've never heard about the Holy Spirit.

> **Paul** | [3]Well then, what kind of ceremonial washing* did you receive?

> **John's Disciples** | We received the ritual cleansing* that John taught.

> **Paul** | [4]John taught the truth—that people should be ritually cleansed* with renewed thinking and turn toward God. But he also taught that the people should believe in the One whose way he was preparing, that is, Jesus.

[5]As soon as they heard this, they were ceremonially washed* again, this time in the name of our Lord Jesus. [6]When Paul laid his hands on them, the Holy Spirit came upon them in the same way the original disciples experienced at Pentecost: they spoke in tongues and prophesied.

19:3 Literally, immersion, a rite of initiation and purification
19:3 Literally, immersion, an act of repentance
19:4 Literally, immersed, in an act of repentance
19:5 Literally, immersed, in a rite of initiation and purification

*B*oth Apollos and this small band of John's disciples heard an incomplete gospel. Our calling is not only to bring the gospel to those who have never heard, but also to expand the truth to those who understand only partial truth. If we see people as they truly are—on a journey to know God—we realize that no one has "arrived." Everyone has something more to learn because we see the truth so dimly.

⁸For three months, Paul continued his standard practice: he went *week by week* to the synagogue, speaking with great confidence, arguing with great persuasiveness, proclaiming the kingdom of God. ⁹⁻¹⁰*Once again*, some members of the synagogue refused to believe and insulted the Way publicly before the whole synagogue community. Paul withdrew and took those with him who had become disciples. For the next two years, he used the public lecture hall of Tyrannus, presenting the Word of the Lord every day, debating with all who would come. As a result, everyone in the region, whether Jews or Greeks, heard the message. ¹¹Meanwhile, God did amazing miracles through Paul. ¹²People would take a handkerchief or article of clothing that had touched Paul's skin and bring it to their sick *friends or relatives*, and the patients would be cured of their diseases or released from the evil spirits that oppressed them.

¹³⁻¹⁴Some itinerant Jewish exorcists *noticed Paul's success in this regard*, so they tried to use the name of Jesus the King in an exorcism they were performing.

Imagine this: there are seven of them, all sons of a Jewish chief priest named Sceva, *gathered around a demonized man in a house.*

One of the Jewish exorcists | I command you to depart, by the Jesus proclaimed by Paul!

Evil Spirit | [15]Jesus I know. Paul I know. But who are you?

[16]Then the man leaps up, attacks them all, rips off their clothing, and beats them so badly that they run out of the house stark naked and covered in bruises.
[17]Word of this strange event spread throughout Ephesus among both Jews and Greeks. Everyone was shocked and realized that the name of Jesus was indeed powerful and praiseworthy. [18]As a result, a number of people involved *in various occult practices* came to faith. They confessed their secret practices and rituals. [19]Some of them had considerable libraries about their magic arts; they piled up their books and burned them publicly. Someone estimated the value of the books to be 50,000 silver coins. [20]Again, word spread, and the message of the Lord overcame resistance and spread powerfully.
[21]Eventually, Paul felt he should move on again. The Holy Spirit confirmed that he should first travel through Macedonia and Achaia and then return to Jerusalem.

Paul | I must eventually see Rome.

[22]So he sent Timothy and Erastus, two of his helpers, ahead to Macedonia while he stayed a while longer in Asia. [23]It was during this time that a major incident occurred involving the Way. [24]*This time, Jews had not caused the disturbance, but Gentiles, and in particular*, an idolmaker named Demetrius. He had a profitable business, for himself and for others, making silver shrines for Artemis *(also known as Diana in Latin), one of the deities worshiped in Ephesus.*

[25]*Picture this:* Demetrius calls a meeting of all the artisans who are similarly employed in idolmaking. *Everyone in the idol industry comes together.*

Demetrius | Men, we are all colleagues in this fine line of work. We're making a good living doing what we're doing. But we'd better wake up, or we're all going to go broke.

[26]You've heard about this fellow Paul. Here in Ephesus, he's already convinced a large number of people to give up using idols. He tells them that our products are worthless. He's been doing this same kind of thing almost everywhere in Asia. [27]It's bad enough that he is slandering our fine and honorable profession, *but do you see where this will lead?* If his lies catch on, the temple of Artemis itself will be called a fraud. The great goddess of our region, the majestic deity who is revered here in Asia and around the world, will be disgraced.

[28]The crowd goes wild with rage. They start chanting.

Crowd | Great is Artemis of the Ephesians! Great is Artemis of the Ephesians!

[29]Soon the whole city is filled with confusion, and a mob forms. They find Paul's Macedonian travel companions, Gaius and Aristarchus, and drag them to the theatre. [30]Paul wants to go confront the crowd and protect his friends, but the disciples hold him back. [31]Even some

provincial officials of Asia who are friendly to Paul send him an urgent message, warning him to stay away from the theatre.

[32]Enraged voices *are shouting on top of each other*, some saying one thing, some saying something else. The crowd is completely out of control. Most of the people don't even know what caused the commotion in the first place. [33]Some of the Jewish people push a man named Alexander to the front of the crowd, hoping he can calm the disturbance. He raises his hands to silence the crowd and gets a few sentences out, [34]but then the crowd realizes he's a Jew *rather than a native Ephesian*, and once again they start chanting.

Crowd | Great is Artemis of the Ephesians!

For two solid hours they keep the chant going.
[35]Finally, the town clerk manages to calm the crowd.

Town Clerk | My fellow citizens of Ephesus, everyone in the world knows that our great city is the caretaker of the temple of Artemis! Everyone knows that we are the home of the great statue that fell from heaven! [36]Our status as the economic center of the idolmaking industry is not in danger, so please, calm down. Don't do anything rash. [37]The men whom you have seized aren't temple robbers, nor have they blasphemed our great goddess. [38]If Demetrius and the artisans who share his important trade have a legal complaint, don't bring it here to the theatre, take it to the courts—they're open today. [39]If you need to charge someone with a crime or launch an inquiry, take the matter to the regional judges. [40]We need to do this according to regulations, or we'll all be charged with rioting. This kind of behavior can't be justified.

⁴¹So he succeeds in dispersing the crowd.

*T*he message of Jesus not only has the power to annihilate economic supremacy, but it can also turn the world upside down in the process. So when the kingdom of God comes is a good time to fine-tune your business plan, because you will not profit from dishonesty, manipulation, or selfishness. In the kingdom of God, a worker is always paid a wage worthy of his work: anyone who works will have enough to eat, and no one will be left out of the profitable bounty of God. May the kingdom come.

PERCHED IN AN OPEN WINDOW

¹As soon as the uproar ended, Paul gathered the disciples together, encouraged them once more, said farewell, and left *on foot*. He decided to pass through Macedonia, ²encouraging believers wherever he found them, and came to Greece. ³He spent three months there, and then planned to set sail once again for Syria. But he learned that a group of Jewish opponents was plotting to kill him, so he decided to travel through Macedonia.

⁴⁻⁵*There was a large group of us traveling with him at this time, and we decided it was best, in light of the plot, to split up and then* reunite in the city of Troas. This group included Paul, a Berean named Sopater (son of Pyrrhus), two Thessalonians named Aristarchus and Secundus, a Derbean named Gaius, two Asians named Tychicus and Trophimus, and Timothy. ⁶Some of us waited until the Days of Unleavened Bread were over; then we went to Philippi where we boarded a ship for Troas. The other group left immediately *on foot, passing through Macedonia*. When my group landed in Troas five days later, Paul's group had already arrived. We stayed in Troas another week.

⁷⁻⁸The Sunday night before our Monday departure, we gathered to celebrate the breaking of bread. *Many wondrous events happened as Paul traveled, ministering among the churches. One evening a most unusual event occurred. Imagine you are celebrating with us:*

We are in an upstairs room, *with the gentle light and shadows* cast by several lamps. Paul is carrying on an extended dialogue with the believers, taking advantage of every moment since we plan to leave at first light. The conversation stretches on until midnight. ⁹A young fellow named Eutychus, seeking some fresh *air*, moves to an open window. Paul keeps on talking. Eutychus perches in the open window itself. *Paul keeps talking*. Eutychus drifts off to sleep. *Paul continues talking* until Eutychus, now overcome by deep sleep, drops out of the window and falls three stories to the ground, where he is found dead. [10]Paul joins us *downstairs*, bends over, and takes Eutychus in his arms.

Paul | It's OK. He's alive again.

[11]Then Paul goes back upstairs, celebrates the breaking of bread, and— *just as you might guess*—keeps on conversing until first light. Then he leaves. [12](I should add that Eutychus had been taken home *long before*, his friends more than a little relieved that the boy was alive!)

*T*his may be one of the strangest stories ever told. Paul is talking about faith while one young man dozes off and falls out the window. Many a pastor has secretly prayed that slumbering congregants would fall out of their chairs. It might have been funny had he not died; instead, it was a scene of great horror. That is, until God used Paul to turn horror into celebration with a death-defying miracle. But the people were so enamored with Paul's teaching about the Liberating King that they returned to their conversations, which lingered until sunrise.

[13]Again, Paul wanted us to split up. He wanted to go by land by himself while we went by ship to Assos. [14]There he came on board with us, and we sailed on to Mitylene. [15]From there we sailed near Chios, passing by it the next day, docking briefly at Samos the day after that, then arriv-

ing at Miletus the following day. ¹⁶This route kept us safely out of
Ephesus and didn't require Paul to spend any time at all in Asia, since
he wanted to arrive in Jerusalem quickly—before Pentecost, he hoped.

¹⁷In Miletus, he sent word to the church in Ephesus, asking the elders to come down to meet with him. ¹⁸When they arrived he said,

Paul | We will have many memories of our time together in
Ephesus, *but of all the memories, most of all I want you to
remember my way of life.* From the first day I arrived in
Asia, ¹⁹I served the Lord with humility and tears,
patiently enduring the many trials that came my way
through the plots of my Jewish opponents. ²⁰I did
everything I could to help you; I held nothing back. I
taught you publicly, and I taught you in your homes. ²¹I
told everyone the same message—Jews and Greeks
alike—that we must repent toward God and have faith
in Jesus our Liberating King. ²²Now, I feel that the
Holy Spirit has taken me captive. I am being led to
Jerusalem. My future is uncertain, ²³but I know—the
Holy Spirit has told me—that everywhere I go from
now on, I will find imprisonment and persecution
waiting for me. ²⁴*But that's OK. That's no tragedy for me
because* I don't cling to my life for my own sake. The
only value I place on my life is that I may finish my
race, that I may fulfill the ministry that Jesus our
King has given me, that I may gladly tell the good
news of God's grace. ²⁵I now realize that this is our
last good-bye. *You have been like family* in all my travels
to proclaim the kingdom of God, but after today none

of you will see my face again. ²⁶So I want to make this clear: I am not responsible for your destiny from this point on ²⁷because I have not held back from telling you the purpose of God in all its dimensions.

²⁸*Here are my instructions:* diligently guard yourselves, and diligently guard the whole flock over which the Holy Spirit has given you oversight. Shepherd the church of God, this precious church which He made His own through the blood of His own Son. ²⁹I know that after I've gone, dangerous wolves will sneak in among you, savaging the flock. ³⁰Some of you here today will begin twisting the truth, enticing disciples to go your way, to follow you. ³¹You must be on guard, and you must remember my way of life among you. For three years I have kept on, persistently warning everyone, day and night, with tears.

³²So now I put you in God's hands. I entrust you to the message of God's grace, a message that has the power to build you up and to give you rich heritage among all who are set apart for God's holy purposes. ³³*Remember my example:* I never once coveted a single coin of silver or gold. I never looked twice at someone's fine clothing. ³⁴No, you know this: I worked with my own two hands *making tents*, and I paid my own expenses and my companions' expenses as well. ³⁵This is my last gift to you, this example of a way of life: a life of hard work, a life of helping the weak, a life that echoes every day those words of Jesus our King, who said, "It is more blessed to give than to receive."

[36]*Once again, imagine this scene:*

As Paul finishes speaking, he kneels down, and we all join him, kneeling. He prays, and we all join him, praying. [37]There's the sound of weeping, and then more weeping, and then more still. One by one we embrace Paul and kiss him, [38]our sadness multiplied because of his words about this being their last good-bye. They walk with us to the ship, *and we set sail.*

*T*he last words of Paul to his disciples are emotional, inspiring, but unbelievably arrogant. Who would place himself on a pedestal and encourage everyone to be more like him? It sounds like a cult of personality, but it is not. Paul understands that the gospel must be incarnate; it is more than a set of ideas, so someone must demonstrate how to walk the path of faith. He calls them to watch him carefully and emulate his behavior: watch how I treat people, how I eat, what I say, the way that I give—and do likewise. If only we possessed the same boldness to say, "do as I do," then the world would be a better place, and we would live with an understanding that we do not just speak the gospel; we are the gospel.

FAREWELL TOUR

¹Cos was our next stop, and the next day, Rhodes, and the next, Patara. ²We found another ship in Patara that would take us *south and east* toward Phoenicia. ³We saw Cyprus to our left and sailed on to Syria, landing at Tyre where the ship had cargo to unload. ⁴We found the disciples there and stayed with them for seven days. The Spirit moved them to tell Paul not to go on to Jerusalem, ⁵but the day came for our departure, and the whole community of disciples, including wives and children, escorted us outside the city. We knelt down together on the beach, prayed together, said farewell, and then parted company—⁶the disciples returning to their homes, we sailing on. ⁷From Tyre we docked at Ptolemais where we met with the believers and spent a day with them. ⁸Then we moved on to Caesarea. In Caesarea, we stayed with Philip the evangelist, one of the seven. ⁹His four virgin daughters lived with him, each having the gift of prophecy. ¹⁰While we were with them, another gifted prophet named Agabus came north from Judea. ¹¹He took Paul's belt and used it to bind his own feet and hands.

> **Agabus** | This is a message from the Holy Spirit: the Jews in Jerusalem will in this way bind the owner of this belt and will hand him over to the Gentiles.

¹²Now we all joined in imploring Paul—we, his companions, *and Philip and his daughters, everyone present*—begging him not to go one step closer to the city. ¹³*Some of us were even crying.*

Paul | Please, you're breaking my heart with your tears! *I know exactly what I'm doing.* I'm fully prepared to be bound, and more—to die for the name of Jesus the King.

¹⁴We realized our persuasion was fruitless, so we stopped pleading with him and simply said, "The Lord's will be done."

*P*aul was a man of great mystery. This persecutor-turned-preacher seemed more like a character from pages of fiction than the instigator of the spread of Christianity. He became what he had once despised and willingly suffered on behalf of his new Savior. Paul was accused of many things, but he was no fool—although he was a fool for Christ. He fully understood what was waiting for him in Jerusalem: persecution, suffering, and ultimately death. His friends begged him not to return to this holy city, but Paul was called to live in the footsteps of the One who was crucified—he was destined to suffer yet called for no drugs. His suffering served a greater purpose, and Paul never lost sight of this spiritual reality. You see, Paul was living in the kingdom of God.

The masses hope for a gospel that makes them happy, healthy, sexy, and wealthy. Jesus said the way of life was a hard road, with only a few on it. Ironically, this hard road will end in life. The easy, broad street—which may be paved with good intentions—will always lead to death and destruction. Which road are you on?

¹⁵So we knew what we were getting into as we prepared to ascend the foothills toward Jerusalem. ¹⁶Some of the disciples from Caesarea

accompanied us and led us to the home of Mnason, a Cypriot and one of the first disciples, with whom we stayed. [17]We continued on to Jerusalem and were welcomed warmly by the brothers there. [18]The next day, we went together to visit James, and all the elders were there with him. [19]Paul greeted them and then reported account after account of what God had done through him among the Gentiles. [20]When they heard his story, they praised God.

James and the Elders | Brother, *we have a problem.* You can see that we have thousands of Jewish believers here, and all of them are zealous law keepers. [21]They've heard all kinds of rumors about you—that you teach all the Jews living among the Gentiles to forget about Moses entirely, that you tell believers not to circumcise their sons, that you teach them to abandon all our customs. [22]We need to deal with this situation, since word will spread that you're here in the city. [23]So here's what we would like you to do. We have four men here who are fulfilling a vow. [24]Join them. Go through the rituals of purification with them. Pay for their heads to be shaved according to our ritual. That will show that the rumors are false and that you are still observing and upholding the law. [25]For the Gentile believers, we've already written in a letter our judgment on their situation: they should not eat food that has been sacrificed to idols, they should not eat meat with blood in it or meat from animals killed by strangulation, and they should abstain from all sexual misconduct.

²⁶Paul complied with their request. The very next day, he publicly joined the four men, completed the initial purification rites, entered the temple with them, and began the *seven-day* ritual purification process, after which a sacrifice would be made for each of them.

²⁷The seven days of purification were almost completed when some Jews from Asia recognized Paul in the temple. They grabbed him.

Asian Jews *(shouting)*	²⁸Help! Fellow Israelites! This man is an enemy of our people, *our religion*, our law, and this temple! He travels around the world subverting our holiest customs! He is at this moment desecrating this holy temple by bringing Gentiles into this sacred place.

²⁹*In this accusation, they were confused*—they had seen Paul elsewhere in the city with Trophimus the Ephesian, and they assumed that one of his current companions was Trophimus. ³⁰*It was too late to clarify, though,* because word spread and soon a huge crowd rushed to the temple. They held Paul and dragged him from the temple and shut the doors behind them. ³¹They *beat* Paul, and it was clear they intended to kill him.

By this time, word of the uproar reached the commandant of the Roman guard assigned to Jerusalem.

³²He led a group of soldiers and officers to the scene. When the mob looked up and saw the soldiers running toward them, they stopped beating Paul. ³³The commandant took him into custody and ordered him to be bound with two chains. He conducted a preliminary interrogation—asking Paul's name, what he had done. ³⁴Members of the crowd were shouting over each other and the tribune couldn't hear a thing, so he ordered Paul to be taken back to the barracks. ³⁵When they

came to the steps leading down from the temple, the crowd was seething with such violence *toward Paul* that the soldiers had to pick him up and carry him. [36]Then the crowd followed.

Crowd | Away with him! *Away with him!*

[37]They were just leaving the temple area when Paul asked the commandant,

Paul | May I say something to you?

Commandant | Do you speak Greek? [38]We thought you were that Egyptian who recently stirred a rebellion and led 4,000 assassins out into the desert. *But if you speak Greek, then obviously you're not the person we supposed.*

Paul | [39]No, I'm a Jew, originally from Tarsus in Cilicia. I'm a citizen from an important city. Please, I beg you, let me speak to the people.

[40]The commandant agreed, and Paul stood there on the steps, motioning for the people to be silent. The crowd settled down, and Paul spoke in their native tongue, Aramaic.

EXPERIENCE WITH THE SUPERNATURAL

Paul | [1]"Brothers and fathers, please let me defend myself against these charges.

[2]When they heard him speaking Aramaic, a hush came over the crowd.

Paul | [3]I am a Jew, born in Tarsus in Cilicia. I was raised here in Jerusalem and was tutored in the great school of Gamaliel. My education trained me in the strict interpretation of the law of our ancestors, and I grew zealous for God, just as all of you are today. [4]I encountered a movement known as the Way, *and I considered it a threat to our religion*, so I persecuted it violently. I put both men and women *in chains*, had them imprisoned, and would have killed them—[5]as the high priest and the entire council of elders will tell you. I received documentation from them to go to Damascus and work with the brothers there to arrest followers of the Way and bring them back to Jerusalem in chains so they could be properly punished. [6]I was on my way to Damascus. It was about noon. Suddenly, a powerful light shone around me, [7]and I fell to the ground. A Voice spoke: "Saul, Saul, why do you persecute Me?" [8]I answered, "Who are You, Lord?" The Voice replied, "I am Jesus of Nazareth, the One you persecute."

[9]My companions saw the light, but they didn't hear

the Voice. ¹⁰I asked, "What do You want me to do, Lord?" The Lord replied, "Get up and go to Damascus; you will be given your instructions there." ¹¹Since the intense light had blinded me, my companions led me by the hand into Damascus. ¹²I was visited there by a devout man named Ananias, a law-keeping Jew who was well spoken of by all the Jews living in Damascus. ¹³He said, "Brother Saul, regain your sight!" I could immediately see again, beginning with Ananias standing before me. ¹⁴Then he said, "You have been chosen by the God of our ancestors to know His will, to see the Righteous One, and to hear the voice of God. ¹⁵You will tell the story of what you have seen and heard to the whole world. ¹⁶So now, don't delay. Get up, be ceremonially cleansed,* and have your sins washed away, as you call on His name *in prayer*."

¹⁷I returned to Jerusalem, and I was praying here in the temple one day. I slipped into a trance ¹⁸and had a vision in which Jesus said to me, "Hurry! Get out of Jerusalem fast! The people here will not receive your testimony about Me." ¹⁹I replied, "But, Lord, they all know that I went from synagogue to synagogue imprisoning and beating everyone who believed in You. ²⁰They know what I was like and how I stood in approval of the execution of Stephen, Your witness, when he was stoned. I even held the coats of those who actually stoned him." ²¹Jesus replied, "Go, for I am going to send you to distant lands to teach the Gentiles."

22:16 Literally, immersed, in a rite of initiation and purification

²²They were listening quietly up until he mentioned *the Gentiles.*

Crowd
(shouting) | Away with him! Such a man can't be allowed to remain here. Kill him! He must die!

²³*Chaos broke out again.* People were shouting, slamming their coats down on the ground, and throwing fistfuls of dust up in the air. ²⁴The commandant ordered the soldiers to bring Paul to the barracks and flog him until he confessed to whatever he had done to stir up this outrage.

²⁵Back at the barracks, as they tied him up with leather thongs, Paul spoke to a nearby officer.

Paul | Is this legal—for you to flog a Roman citizen without a trial?

²⁶The officer went and spoke to the commandant.

Officer | What can you do about this? Did you know this fellow is a Roman citizen?

Commandant
(rushing to Paul's side) | ²⁷What's this? Are you really a Roman citizen?

Paul | Yes.

Commandant | ²⁸I paid a small fortune for my citizenship.

Paul | I was born a citizen.

²⁹Hearing this, those who were about to start the flogging pulled back, and the commandant was concerned because he had arrested and bound a citizen *without cause*. ³⁰He still needed to conduct an investigation to uncover the Jews' accusations against Paul. So the next day he removed the ties on Paul and called a meeting with the chief priests and council of elders. He brought Paul in and had him stand before the group.

*T*hese Jewish leaders are prepared to fight and squabble with Paul about the Law. But, in his wisdom, Paul disarms them with his story. He is one of them, and on his journey to defend Judaism against these Christian heretics, he encountered the living God. How can anyone dispute his experience? He was trained by trustworthy Jews and lived his life according to their strict interpretation of the Law. When Paul invites us into his experience with the supernatural, it makes debating the finer points of the Law seem ridiculous. It would be like antagonizing Moses while he reiterated God's message heard through the burning bush. But prejudice is apparently stronger than any divine message. Paul has them hanging on to every word from his mouth, until he speaks of the Gentiles. The crowd immediately rises from their silence into a furious rage. The message is clear—if your revelation extends beyond our people, we will hear nothing of it. How could all of these students of the Hebrew Scriptures have been so ignorant about God's intentions to liberate all people? The prophets had declared God's plan to offer grace to Jews and non-Jews, but no one in this crowd considered that good news.

THE NERVE OF YOU!

¹Paul stared at the council and spoke:

> **Paul** | Brothers, I have always lived my life to this very day with a clear conscience before God.

²Ananias the high priest signaled those standing near Paul to hit him on the mouth.

> **Paul** | ³You hypocrite! God will slap you! How dare you sit in judgment and claim to represent the law, while you violate the law by ordering me to be struck *for no reason?*

> **Bystanders** | The nerve of you insulting the high priest of God!

> **Paul** | ⁵I'm sorry, my brothers. I didn't realize this was the high priest. The law warns us to not curse the ruler of the people.*

⁶Paul noticed that some members of the council were Sadducees and some were Pharisees, so he quickly spoke to the council.

> **Paul** | Brothers, I am a Pharisee, born to a Pharisee. I am on trial because I have hope that the dead are raised!

23:5 Exodus 22:28

[7]That got the two parties arguing with one another, [8]because the Sadducees say there is no such thing as resurrection, angels, or spirits, and the Pharisees believe in all three.

[9]Soon these leaders were shouting, and some of the scholars from the party of the Pharisees rose to their feet.

Pharisees | There is nothing wrong with this man. Maybe he really has encountered a spirit or an angel.

[10]The two parties were about to start throwing punches, and the commandant was afraid Paul would be torn to pieces, so he sent in his soldiers to intervene. They took Paul back into custody and returned him to their barracks. [11]That night the Lord came near and spoke to him.

*P*aul is brilliant. If you are accused by a group of religious intellectuals, the smartest thing to do is to get them fighting with one another. Paul understood the axiom, "the enemy of my enemy is my friend." So if I pick a fight with the Sadducees, the rest of the room will defend me. The things we are against often define us, so we are easily manipulated in this way. Consider some of the conservative political pundits who have never espoused any inclination toward Christianity. They gain millions of Christian followers by opposing the political enemies of conservative Christians. Paul embraced a similar strategy here—if I can get these guys to fight, they will forget why we are actually here. In many ways the culture wars have served the same purpose. In the middle of the battle the church is realizing we were not placed on earth to fight about morality and culture. We are here to

> bring the kingdom of God to earth. His kingdom will not come by means of legislation, but by the working of the Holy Spirit within the church.

The Lord | Keep up your courage, Paul! You have successfully told your story about Me in Jerusalem, and soon you will do the same in Rome.

[12-13]That morning a group of more than 40 Jewish opponents conspired to kill Paul. *They* bound themselves by an oath that they wouldn't eat or drink until he was dead. [14]They told the chief priests and elders about their plan.

Jewish Opponents | We've made an oath not to eat or drink until this man is dead. [15]So you and the council must ask the commandant to bring Paul to meet with you. Tell him that you want to further investigate Paul's case. We'll get rid of *the troublemaker* on his way here.

[16]Now Paul had a nephew who heard about the planned ambush; he managed to gain entry into the barracks and alerted Paul. [17]Paul called one of the officers.

Paul | Take this young man to the commandant. He has news the commandant needs to hear.

[18]The officer took him to the commandant.

Officer | The prisoner named Paul asked me to bring this man to you. He has some kind of information.

[19]The commandant led him away so they could speak in private.

Commandant | What do you want to tell me?

Young Man | [20-21]The Jewish council is going to ask you to bring Paul down to the council tomorrow under the pretext that there will be a thorough examination. But don't agree to do it, because 40 assassins have bound themselves to an oath not to eat or drink until they've killed Paul. Their plan is in motion, and they're simply waiting for you to play your part.

[22]The commandant sent the young man home with these instructions: "Don't tell a soul that you've spoken with me." [23]Then he called for two officers.

Commandant | At nine o'clock tonight, you will leave for Caesarea with 200 soldiers, 70 horsemen, and 200 spearmen. [24]Have a mount for Paul to ride and conduct him safely to Felix the governor.

[25]He wrote the following letter:

[26]*Commandant* Claudius Lysias greets his excellency, Felix, Governor. [27]The accompanying prisoner was seized by Jews who were about to kill him. I learned he was a Roman citizen and intervened with the guard

here to protect him. [28]I arranged for a hearing before their council [29]and learned that he was accused for reasons relating to their religious law, but that he has done nothing deserving imprisonment or execution. [30]I was informed that a group was planning to assassinate him, so I sent him to you immediately. I will require his accusers to present their complaint before you.

[31]So the soldiers followed their orders and safely conducted Paul as far as Antipatris that night. [32-33]The next day, the horsemen conducted him on to Caesarea as the foot soldiers returned to the barracks. The horsemen delivered the letter and the prisoner to Felix who read the letter. [34]The only question Felix asked concerned the province of Paul's birth. When he learned Paul was from Cilicia, [35]he said,

Felix | As soon as your accusers arrive I will hear your case.

He placed Paul under guard within Herod's headquarters.

Acts 24

ULTIMATE JUSTICE

¹The high priest Ananias came north *to Caesarea* five days later, accompanied by some elders and an attorney named Tertullus. They explained their case to Felix *without Paul present.* ²When Paul was brought in, Tertullus launched into an accusation.

Tertullus | Most Excellent Felix, through your esteemed leadership we have enjoyed a long and happy peace. Your foresight in governance has brought many reforms for the people I represent. ³We always and everywhere welcome every thought of you with high and deep gratitude. ⁴But, knowing how busy you are and how limited your time must be, I beg you to hear us briefly present our case to you with the legendary graciousness for which you are known everywhere.

⁵Here are the facts: this man is a disease to the body politic. He agitates trouble in Jewish communities throughout our empire as a ringleader of the *heretical* sect known as the Nazarenes. ⁶He even tried to desecrate the temple, so we seized him. [Our aim was to try him by the Jewish law. ⁷But Commandant Lysias interfered and removed this man from our control. ⁸Because of his meddling you are now forced to hear those making the accusation.*] You will find, through your own examination, that everything we say of Paul is true.

24:6-8 This portion of verses 6-8 is omitted from some ancient manuscripts.

⁹The Jewish opponents present added their vigorous testimony in support of the lawyer's opening statement. ¹⁰The governor *didn't say anything*, but he motioned for Paul to speak.

Paul | I am happy now to make my defense to you, sir, knowing that you have been a judge over this nation for many years. ¹¹Just twelve days ago I went up to Jerusalem to worship, as you can easily verify. ¹²I wasn't arguing with anyone in the temple. I wasn't stirring up a crowd in any of the synagogues. I wasn't disturbing the peace of the city in any way. They did not find me doing these things in Jerusalem, ¹³nor can they prove that I have done any of the things of which they have accused me. ¹⁴But I can make this confession: I believe everything established by the Law and written in the Prophets, and I worship the God of our ancestors according to the Way, which they call a *heretical* sect.

¹⁵*Here is my crime:* I have a hope in God that there will be a resurrection of both the just and unjust, which my opponents also share. ¹⁶Because of this hope, I always do my best to live with a clear conscience toward God and all people. ¹⁷I have been away for several years, so recently I brought gifts for the poor of my nation and offered sacrifices. ¹⁸When they found me I was not disturbing anyone, nor was I gathering a crowd. No, I was quietly completing the rite of purification. Some Jews from Asia *are the ones who started the disturbance*—¹⁹and if they have an accusation, they should be here to make it. ²⁰If these men here have

some crime they have found me guilty of when I stood before their council, they should present it. [21]Perhaps my crime is that I spoke this one sentence in my testimony before them: "I am on trial here today because I have hope that the dead are raised."

[22]Felix was quite knowledgeable about the Way. He adjourned the preliminary hearing.

> **Felix** | When Lysias the commandant comes *to Caesarea*, I will decide your case.

[23]He then ordered the officer to keep Paul in custody, but to permit him some freedom and to allow any of his friends to take care of his needs.

[24]A few days later, Felix sent for Paul and gave him an opportunity to speak about faith in Jesus as Liberating King. Felix was accompanied by his wife Drusilla, who was Jewish. [25]As Paul spoke of justice, self-control, and the coming judgment, Felix became agitated.

> **Felix** | That's enough for now. When I have time, I will send for you again.

[26]They had a number of conversations of this sort, *but Felix's motives were not as sincere as they might seem.* He actually was hoping that by having frequent contact, Paul might offer him a bribe. [27]As a favor to the Jews, he did nothing to resolve the case and left Paul in prison for two years. Then Felix completed his assignment as governor, and Porcius Festus succeeded him.

*T*here were rumors that a large sum of money was at Paul's disposal. We know that money was the relief offering for the church in Jerusalem. But Paul did not choose to buy his freedom. Despite the corruption of the government, Paul understood that ultimately his justice was in the hands of God. In the near future, he would appear before the government of Rome, and that encounter would likely lead to his death.

Acts 25

SO TO THE EMPEROR YOU WILL GO

¹Three days after arriving in the province, Festus traveled south from Caesarea to Jerusalem. ²⁻³The chief priests and Jewish leaders still had a plan to kill Paul and gave a report to Festus about their unresolved grievances against Paul. They suggested that as a favor to them, Festus should move Paul to Jerusalem. Of course, this was part of the plan to set an ambush for Paul and kill him en route. ⁴Festus *instead offered to reopen the case.* He would be going back to Caesarea soon.

Festus | ⁵So let your leaders accompany me and bring your accusations against the man.

⁶Eight or ten days later Festus returned to Caesarea, and the next day took his seat in court. He ordered Paul to be brought before him. ⁷The Jewish opponents from Jerusalem immediately surrounded Paul and from all directions bombarded him with all sorts of serious charges, none of which could be proven.

Paul
(quietly and simply) | ⁸In no way have I committed any offense against Jewish law, against the Jewish temple and all it represents, or against the emperor.

⁹Here Festus saw an opportunity to do just the favor Paul's Jewish opponents had requested.

Festus | Would you like to have your trial in Jerusalem? I'd be willing to try your case there.

Paul | [10-11]*Sir, it's not that I'm afraid to die.* If I had committed a capital offense, I would accept my punishment. But I'm sure it's clear to you that I have done no wrong to the Jews. Since their charges against me are completely empty, it would be wrong to turn me over to them. *No, I do not wish to go to Jerusalem.* I am appealing to the court of the emperor in Rome.

[12]Festus conferred privately with his council and returned with this decision:

Festus | You have appealed to the emperor, so to the emperor you will go.

[13]Several days later, the provincial king Agrippa arrived in Caesarea with his wife Bernice to welcome the new governor. [14]Their visit lasted several days, which gave Festus the chance to describe Paul's case.

Festus | Felix left me some unfinished business involving a prisoner *named Paul.* [15]When I was in Jerusalem, I got an earful about him from the chief priests and Jewish elders. They wanted me simply to decide against him, [16]but I informed them that we Romans don't work that way. We don't condemn a person accused of a crime unless the accusers present their case in person so the accused has ample opportunity to defend himself against the charge. [17]I arranged for them to come here for a proper hearing. In fact, the first day after I returned to Caesarea, I took my seat in court and heard his case without delay. [18]Contrary to my expectations, the accusers brought no substantial charges against him at all. [19]Instead, they were bickering about their own religious beliefs related to a fellow named Jesus, who had died, but whom Paul claimed was raised to life again. [20]I had no idea how to handle a religious squabble pretending to be a legal case, so I suggested Paul be taken to Jerusalem so he could be tried on Jewish turf, so to speak. [21]But Paul refused, and instead he appealed to be kept in custody so the case could be referred to his Imperial Majesty. So I have held him until we can arrange to send him to the emperor.

Agrippa | [22]This sounds interesting. I'd like to hear this fellow in person.

Festus | You will, then. We'll bring him in tomorrow.

[23]The next day, King Agrippa and Bernice arrived at the great hall with great formality, accompanied by the military commanders and the city's leading men. Festus ordered Paul to be brought before them.

Festus | [24]King Agrippa and all our honored guests, here is the man who has been charged with wrongdoing by the Jewish community—both in Jerusalem and here. They yelled for his execution, [25]but I found him guilty of no capital offense. Then he appealed to our Imperial Majesty, so I have agreed that he will be sent to Rome. [26-27]*Here is where I need your help.* I can't send a man to our emperor without a letter logically detailing the charges against him, but I have no idea what to write. So, King Agrippa, and all of you honored guests, I'm requesting your help in determining what to write in my letter to the emperor.

Acts 26

Agrippa | ¹Go ahead. You may speak for yourself.
(to Paul) |

Paul | ²I am indeed fortunate to be standing before you, King
(extending his hand) | Agrippa, to humbly defend myself against accusations
from my Jewish opponents. ³You are extraordinarily
familiar with Jewish customs and controversies, so I
beg your patience as I begin. ⁴My way of life is well
known to the whole Jewish community, how I have
lived in the Jewish community abroad and in
Jerusalem. ⁵If they are willing to speak, they themselves will tell you something they have long known—
that I was a member of the strictest sect of our religion and lived for many years as a Pharisee. ⁶But now I
am on trial here *for this simple reason:* I have hope. I
have hope rooted in a promise God made to our ancestors. ⁷All our twelve tribes have hope in this promise—
they express their hope as they worship day and
night. How strange it is, then, Your Excellency, that I
am accused by the Jews of having hope! ⁸Why would
any of you think it is absurd to have hope that God
raises the dead? ⁹As you know, we're talking specifically about Jesus of Nazareth. For a long time I was convinced that I should work against that name. ¹⁰I
opposed it in Jerusalem. I received authorization from
the chief priests to lock many of His followers in

prison. When they were threatened with execution, I voted against them. [11]I would find them in synagogues across Jerusalem and try to force them to blaspheme. My fury drove me to pursue them to foreign cities as well.

[12]On one occasion, I was traveling to Damascus, authorized and commissioned by the chief priests *to find and imprison more of His followers.* [13]It was about midday, Your Excellency, when I saw a light from heaven—brighter than the noonday sun—shining around my companions and me. [14]We all fell to the ground in fear, and I then heard a Voice. The words were in Aramaic: "Saul, Saul, why are you persecuting Me? When you kick against the cattle prods, you're only hurting yourself." [15]I asked, "Lord, who are You?" and the Lord answered, "I am Jesus, the One you are persecuting. [16]Get up now and stand upright on your feet. I have appeared to you for a reason. I am appointing you to serve Me. You are to tell My story and how you have now seen Me, and you are to continue to tell the story in the future. [17]I will rescue you from your Jewish opponents and from the Gentiles—for it is to the Gentiles I am sending you. [18]It will be your mission to open their eyes so that they may turn from darkness to light and from the kingdom of Satan to the kingdom of God. This is so that they may receive forgiveness of all their sins and have a place among those who are set apart for a holy purpose through having faith in Me."

¹⁹King Agrippa, I did not disobey this vision from heaven. ²⁰I began in Damascus, then continued in Jerusalem, then throughout the Judean countryside, then among the Gentiles—telling everyone they must turn from their past and toward God, and they must align their deeds and way of life with this new direction. ²¹So then, this is my crime. This is why my Jewish opponents seized me that day in the temple and tried to kill me. ²²God has helped me right up to this very moment, so I can stand here telling my story to both the humble and the powerful alike. I only say what the prophets and Moses said would happen—²³that God's Liberating King must suffer, and then, by being the first to rise from the dead, He would proclaim light to both Jews and Gentiles.

Festus
(interrupting) | ²⁴You've gone crazy, Paul! You've read one book too many and have gone insane!

Paul | ²⁵No, most excellent Festus, I am not insane. I am telling the sane and sober truth. ²⁶The king understands what I'm talking about, which is why I could speak so freely to him. None of these things have been covered up and hidden away in a corner, so I'm sure none of these things have escaped his notice. ²⁷King Agrippa, do you believe the prophets? I know you must believe.

Agrippa | ²⁸Paul, have you so quickly moved on from defending yourself to trying to persuade me to become a Christian?

Paul | ²⁹Whether I have done so quickly or not, I pray to God that not only you but also everyone who is listening to me today might become what I am—minus these chains.

³⁰The king stood to leave at this point, and the governor, Bernice, and all those who had been seated, ³¹and as they left, everyone was saying the same thing: "This man isn't doing anything deserving death—he shouldn't even be in prison."

Agrippa | ³²This man could have been released completely if he
(to Festus) | had not appealed to the emperor.

ALL 276!

¹The date was set for us to depart for Rome, and Paul and some other prisoners were transferred to the custody of a Roman officer named Julius, a member of the Augustan Division. *²I was permitted to join Paul for his journey to Rome*, along with Aristarchus, a Macedonian brother from Thessalonica. We boarded a ship from Adramyttium that was stopping in ports along the coast of Asia. ³We stopped the next day at Sidon, and Julius kindly allowed Paul to visit friends and be taken care of by them. ⁴We sailed from there north of Cyprus because the winds were unfavorable. ⁵We passed Cilicia and Pamphylia *on our right* and then came to Myra in Lycia. ⁶There, Julius found a ship from Alexandria heading directly to Italy, to which we transferred. ⁷The winds were still contrary, so we made slow progress for a number of days and with difficulty passed Cnidus and sailed south toward Crete and past Cape Salmone *on its eastern end*. ⁸Sailing conditions were adverse to say the least. Finally, we came to a place called Fair Havens, near the city of Lasea *on the south coast of Crete*. ⁹We had lost a lot of time already—it was *late in the year for sailing—following the Day of Atonement* and conditions had deteriorated from adverse to dangerous. Paul tried to warn those in charge.

> **Paul** | ¹⁰Sirs, if we proceed, I can see that our voyage will be dangerous and will involve heavy loss, not only of cargo, but of the ship itself; not only of the ship, but also of our lives.

[11]But the officer ignored Paul and instead trusted the ship's pilot and owner who felt they could proceed.

[12]*We had two choices.* We could anchor in the harbor at Fair Havens and spend the winter, or we could proceed *west along the coastline,* hoping to reach Phoenix and wait there for calmer spring weather. *Fair Havens* was not a good option, though, being vulnerable to winter storms, so most of us agreed we should try to reach Phoenix, whose harbor was more protected. [13]One day, a moderate south wind began to blow, which made an attempt possible. We weighed anchor and sailed *west,* staying near shore. [14]*Then things got scary.* A violent *northeaster,* the Euraquilo, blew down across Crete. [15]We were caught. We couldn't turn and sail into this fierce wind, so we had no choice but to let it drive us. [16]We briefly found a bit of shelter from the wind near the island of Clauda. We had been having trouble securing the ship's lifeboat, [17]but we were able there to hoist it up and send down cables to brace the hull, *which was in danger of breaking apart under the strain of the storm.* But the wind was relentless and soon we were again being driven southwest, at the mercy of the storm. We feared it would drive us all the way to the Syrtis Banks, *down near the North African coast,* so we threw out the sea anchor to slow us down. *All through the night, the storm pounded us violently.* [18]The next day the crew threw the ship's cargo overboard, [19]and the day after that they discarded any of the ship's equipment they could do without. [20]Days passed without relief from the furious winds, without a single break in the clouds to see sun or stars, even for a moment. Despair set in, as if all hope rescue had been cast overboard as well. [21]On top of all of this, the crew had been unable to eat anything because of the turmoil. *Paul saw the crew had reached a critical moment.* He gathered them.

Paul | Men, if you had listened to my warning, we would still be safe in Crete and we would have avoided this damage and loss. *22I was correct in my warning,* so I urge you to believe me now: none of you will die. We will lose the ship, but we will not lose one life. So keep up your courage, men! 23The God I belong to, the God I worship, sent an angelic messenger to me this night. 24He said, "Do not be afraid, Paul. *I'm not finished with you yet.* You are going to stand before the emperor! You can be certain that God has granted safety to you and all your companions." 25So listen, men: *you must not give up hope!* Keep up your courage! I have faith in God that things will turn out exactly as I was told last night. *26Here's what I foresee:* we will run aground on some island.

27-28Imagine what happened: It's the 14th night *of our nightmare* voyage; we're being driven by the storm somewhere in the Adriatic Sea. It's about midnight, and the sailors are taking soundings, fearing we might run aground. "Twenty fathoms," somebody calls out in the darkness, then a little later, "Fifteen fathoms." *Suddenly you can feel a moment of hope among the crew—* we're nearing land! 29But hope quickly gives way to a new fear. At any moment in this darkness, they realize, we could be smashed onto unseen rocks. So they drop four anchors from the stern and pray for first light.

30Then some of the crew decide to make a run for it on their own. They say they need to let out more anchors from the bow, and this will require lowering the ship's lifeboat. *They actually plan to abandon us; we realize what's going on.* 31Paul quickly speaks to the officer and soldiers.

Paul | Unless these men stay on board, you won't survive.

[32]So the soldiers intervene, cut away the lifeboat, and let it drift away. [33]We wait.

Just before dawn, Paul again gathers everyone on the ship—*all 276 of us*. He urges everyone to eat *and encourages us not to lose hope*.

> **Paul** | Listen, men, we've all been under incredible stress for 14 days. You haven't eaten anything during this whole time. [34]I urge you to take some food now because it will help you survive what we're about to face. And I want to assure you—not one of you will lose a single hair from your head. *We're all going to make it—all 276 of us!*

[35]Then Paul takes a loaf of bread and gives thanks to God in front of all of them. He breaks it, takes a piece, and begins to eat. [36-37]A fresh surge of courage seems to fill their hearts as they also begin to eat. [38]After satisfying their hunger, the crew lightens the ship by throwing the remaining wheat overboard. [39]Day finally breaks. They survey the coastline and don't recognize it, but they do notice a bay with a beach—the best place to try to run ashore.

[40]So they cut the anchor ropes, untie the steering oars, hoist the foresail to the wind, and make for the beach. [41]But *then there's a horrible sound,* and we realize we've struck a reef; the bow is jammed solid, and the waves are smashing the stern to pieces. [42]The soldiers start talking about killing the prisoners so they won't swim away and escape, [43]but the officer wants to save Paul so he stops them. He tells those who can swim to jump overboard and swim to the shore, [44]and those who can't, he tells to hold on to planks and other pieces of the ship when it breaks apart. *Some hours later*, we reassemble on the beach, each one safe and sound.

Acts 28

THE ULTIMATE AUTHORITY

¹We quickly learned that we were on the island of Malta. ²The Maltese people found us and were extraordinarily kind to us. They kindled a bonfire and welcomed us around it, which we greatly appreciated because it was raining and cold. ³Paul was gathering firewood and helping build the fire. A viper had been hiding in some of the wood and as it tried to escape the heat, it bit Paul on the hand. It sank its fangs in and wouldn't let go. ⁴The natives saw it dangling from his hand.

> **Natives** | This man must be a murderer. He escaped the sea, but now justice has caught up with him.

⁵Paul simply shook the snake off into the fire and suffered no harm. ⁶The natives knew what to expect—rapid swelling followed by death—but when they waited a long time and saw that Paul suffered no ill effects of the bite, they changed their minds and concluded that he was a god.

⁷The leading man of the island, Publius, owned large amounts of land near this beach. Publius received us and hosted us for three days. ⁸Publius's father was sick, bedridden with fever and dysentery. Paul visited the invalid and prayed for him, placing his hands on Publius's father. The man was cured. ⁹Soon, people from all over the island who had diseases came, and they were cured as well.

¹⁰⁻¹¹We stayed on Malta for the next three months and were treated with great honor. When *spring* arrived, we prepared to continue our journey on a ship that had wintered there—an Alexandrian vessel with

the Twin Brothers as its figurehead. The Maltese people showed us a final kindness as we departed: they came with all the provisions we needed for our journey and put them on board.

¹²⁻¹³We *set sail from Malta* and stopped first at Syracuse. After three days, we weighed anchor and came to Rhegium. We waited there a day, and then a south wind sprang up and sped us to Puteoli. ¹⁴We found some believers there, and they invited us to stay with them for seven days. Then we reached Rome. ¹⁵The believers from Rome heard we were coming, so they traveled out to meet us at the Forum of Appius and Three Taverns. Paul thanked God and felt encouraged to see them. ¹⁶Once inside the city, Paul lived under house arrest by himself, with only one soldier to guard him.

¹⁷Three days after his arrival, he called together the local Jewish leaders.

Paul | Brothers, although I committed no wrong against our Jewish people or our ancestral customs, I was arrested in Jerusalem and handed over to the Romans. ¹⁸The Romans examined me and wanted to set me free because I had committed no capital offense. ¹⁹But my Jewish opponents objected, so I had to appeal to the emperor—even though I had no charges against me and had filed no charges against my nation. ²⁰I wanted to gather you together and explain all this to you. I want you to understand that it is because of Israel's hope that I am bound with this chain.

Jewish Leaders | ²¹We haven't received letters from Judea about you, and no visiting brother has reported anything or said anything negative about you. ²²So we are interested in hearing your viewpoint on the sect *you represent*. The only thing we know about it is that people everywhere speak against it.

²³They scheduled a day to meet again, and a large number came to his lodging. From morning until evening, he explained his message to them—giving his account of the kingdom of God, trying to convince them about Jesus from the law of Moses and the prophets' writings. ²⁴Some were convinced, but others refused to believe.

Paul
(added as they left in disagreement)

The Holy Spirit rightly spoke to your ancestors through the prophet Isaiah,

²⁶Go to this people and say:
"You certainly do hear, but you will never understand;
You certainly do see, but you will never have insight.
²⁷Make their hearts hard,
And their ears deaf,
And their eyes blind.
Otherwise, they would look and see,
Listen and hear,
Understand and repent,
And be healed."*

²⁸So let it be known to you that God's liberation, *God's healing*, has been sent to the Gentiles, and they will listen.

28:26-27 Isaiah 6:9-10

[²⁹Then the local Jewish leaders left Paul to discuss all he had told them.*]

³⁰For two full years he lived there in Rome, paying all his own expenses, receiving all who came to him. ³¹With great confidence and with no hindrance, he proclaimed the kingdom of God and taught about *the ultimate authority*, Jesus, the promised Liberating King.

*L*uke's account of the early church ends on a flat note: one of the story's heroes, Paul, is under house arrest in Rome awaiting trial. If we wish to know what happens next, we have to turn to other sources. Although we don't know the details of his captivity, we do learn that Paul was martyred in Rome, a victim of Nero's paranoia and cruelty.

We don't know why Luke left the story when he did. Some think he planned a third volume. Others speculate that he wrote this before Paul's demise—he too was waiting to find out what would happen. It is a possibility, given the uncertainties of life, that our author could not resolve the story because of imprisonment, illness, or his own death. What seems most likely is that Luke finished what he started. He was determined to trace "the Way" as it moved geographically and cultural-ly from Jerusalem (at the edge of the empire) to Rome (the celebrated center of the world). And he did just that.

As it moved geographically, "the Way," as Jesus' followers pre-ferred to call it, had to cross cultural, linguistic, and religious bound-aries. At each and every point, Luke assures, the Spirit was there demonstrating God's blessing on and approval for the apostles who walked in the footsteps of Jesus and in fulfillment of prophecies.

28:29 some of the earliest and best manuscripts do not contain verse 29.

Clearly, what happened in those early decades was driven by the Spirit-wind of heaven. No human could have done alone what the Jewish followers of Jesus did when they left Jerusalem to become the church, comprised of people from every tribe, every ethnicity, every language. Still, Luke is quick to remind us that God's purposes were realized through the faithful obedience of disciples like Peter, Stephen, Philip, and Paul.

Luke's account may have ended, but the story about the acts of God through the church continues into our day. We are the characters in the current volume of salvation history. Through our faithful obedience, empowered by the Spirit-wind of heaven, the plot is developing in our day until our stories are compiled into the wider story of God's new creation.

Section Two // **The Evolving Church in Acts**

THE SEQUEL TO THE GOSPEL OF LUKE

by Robert Creech

Beloved Theophilus

Retelling the story for a new time and audience provides a fresh perspective. Luke originally addressed the story of Jesus and His community to someone named "Theophilus" (Luke 1:1-4; Acts 1:1-2). Who was he? Historical approaches futilely attempted to identify Theophilus, offering as many as a dozen theories about who this shadowy figure might be. The structural study of narrative (narratology) offers a different perspective, however, because it proceeds with different questions.

Narratives always have a *narrator*, the "voice that tells the story," and a *recipient*, the "reader in the text" to whom the story is addressed.[1] Often the reader is unnamed, as in Matthew, Mark, and John. Even then the recipient is present, however. What the narrator explains or leaves unexplained, the languages used, the places named, and the people introduced all testify to what the receiver of the narration may be assumed to know. A composite picture can be drawn of the recipient using these details. In this way we can get to know Theophilus.[2]

A careful reading of Luke-Acts reveals Theophilus to be a "God-fearer," one of those Gentiles on the fringe of the synagogue who is attracted to the God of Israel, but who has yet to become a full convert. He speaks Greek, not Aramaic. Luke is careful not to use Aramaic names for people or places without translating them, and he often substitutes Greek words where Matthew and Mark use Aramaic or Hebrew.

Theophilus is unfamiliar with Palestine. Details must be explained to him. He does not know, for instance, that Nazareth is a city in Galilee or that it was built on a cliff. He does not know that Judah is in the hill country, that

---

1 Gerald Prince, "Introduction to the Study of the Narratee," in *Reader-Response Criticism: From Formalism to Post-Structuralism*, ed. Jane P. Tompkins (Baltimore: Johns Hopkins University Press, 1980), p. 7.

2 For a thorough treatment of Theophilus as the recipient in Luke-Acts, see my essay, "Most Excellent Narratee: The Significance of Theophilus in Luke-Acts," in *With Steadfast Purpose: Essays on Acts in Honor of Henry Jackson Flanders, Jr.*, edited by Raymond H. Keathley (Waco: Baylor University, 1990).

Bethlehem is the city of David, or that Capernaum is in the region of Galilee. Theophilus is unaware that the country of the Gerasenes is opposite Galilee and that Bethany and Bethphage are near the mountain called Olivet. He is unfamiliar with the village of Emmaus and with its distance from Jerusalem. Luke regularly offers Theophilus assistance in understanding such geographical references in Palestine.

On the other hand, Theophilus is broadly familiar with the Roman world. Luke can mention many of those place names without explanation. Theophilus is not as widely traveled as our narrator, however. He does not know the details of many of the places mentioned. He is unaware that Lystra houses a temple to Zeus and that Philippi is both a leading city of Macedonia and a Roman colony. Although he knows of Thessalonica, he is not familiar with the synagogue in that city. His knowledge of Athens does not include an awareness of the extent of its idolatry or of the customs of the Athenian philosophers. He does not know that Fair Havens is near the city of Lasea or that Phoenix is a harbor of Crete facing southwest and northwest. Theophilus does not know about the island of Claudia or details of Malta. He is familiar, however, with the environs of Rome, such as the Market of Appius and the Three Inns.

Theophilus is a spiritually oriented man. (His name means "lover of God.") He is familiar with, or at least ready to accept as valid, a wide variety of religious experiences. He does not need to be convinced about the reality of angels or visions. He receives references to demon exorcism and occult practices without further explanation. He is willing to accept accounts of miracles and understands the practice of prayer and worship. Luke offers, without apology, accounts of unusual, mystical experiences. Theophilus does not need the narrator to explain for him the role of prophecy or to argue for its validity. He is also acquainted with that experience of the Divine marked by fear and awe.

Besides being familiar with the language of religious experience, Theophilus also knows Judaism's essential features. He is acquainted in general with the priesthood and temple of Jerusalem, but he lacks knowledge of some details. He needs no explanation of the personnel and practices of the synagogue. Luke provides him no assistance in understanding an assortment of Jewish terms. He is acquainted with the Feast of Passover, although he must be told that it is the same as the Feast of Unleavened Bread and the day of the offering of the Passover sacrifice. Theophilus understands the Jewish significance of Pentecost as well. Theophilus is acquainted with Sabbath practices. Circumcision is mentioned often, especially in Acts, so Theophilus must understand its significance. The only commentary accompanying a reference to circumcision is in the instance of Timothy. There, the narrator must make it clear to Theophilus why Timothy should be circumcised when the Jerusalem leadership had concluded that the rite was not essential to Christian faith.

Luke cites the Scriptures of the Old Testament frequently, assuming Theophilus will recognize their identity and authority. He introduces Israel's hope for a Messiah in his Gospel, and he refers to it often in Acts without a word of explanation. Although Theophilus knows of Jewish sects, he needs some additional details about the Sadducees and Pharisees. He is not surprised to hear accounts of Gentiles who worship the God of Israel, and he knows the term "God-fearing" without its being defined.

Luke assumes practically no knowledge of Christianity on the part of Theophilus, however. In the Gospel preface, he expresses his intent to write an "orderly account" of the things that had taken place so that Theophilus might know the exact truth "on the things you have been taught." This meta-narrative explanation raises an important issue concerning the reader in the text: is he or is he not a Christian reader? Is he to be included in the "us" of Luke 1:1-2? What had he been taught?

In narratology, the recipient is ignorant of the facts of the narrative until they are presented to him. To compensate for his abysmal ignorance, however, the reader possesses a sure memory of all events in the narrative once he has heard them.[3] In Acts, for example, Luke may assume that Theophilus remembers all the events narrated in his Gospel. Jesus and His disciples do not have to be reintroduced. But the knowledge that Theophilus possesses in the Gospel is considerably less.[4]

In the Gospel, Theophilus knows neither John the Baptist nor Jesus, so he must hear the stories of their birth and childhood. Mary and Joseph must be introduced. He does not know of Jesus' birth in Bethlehem or when it occurred. He is unaware of when the ministries of John and Jesus began. Theophilus is

---

3 Prince, "Introduction," p. 10.

4 The assumed ignorance of the recipient of Luke might be contrasted with the knowledge one must assume on the part of the reader of the Fourth Gospel (R. Alan Culpepper, *Anatomy of the Fourth Gospel* (Minneapolis, MN: Augsburg Fortress Press, 1987, p. 224).

uninformed about Jesus' lineage and how it relates to the history of Israel and of humankind. He must learn about the growth of opposition against Jesus, and how, though innocent, Jesus could be executed by Rome as a criminal. Luke also must lead Theophilus to hear the testimony of those to whom Jesus appeared after His resurrection. In the Gospel, the narrator addresses Theophilus as if he knew nothing of Jesus' birth, life, teaching, death, and resurrection.

In Acts, Theophilus's ignorance surrounds the beginnings and growth of the Christian movement. Every figure that does not appear in the Gospel's narrative must be introduced in Acts. A few names appear with such little fanfare that we might assume Theophilus has heard of them: James of Jerusalem, Jason, Alexander, Herod Agrippa II, and Bernice. In general, however, the names associated with the beginnings of the early church are new information for Theophilus.

The recipient of Acts must learn about the death of Judas and the selection of his successor. He must be instructed concerning the events on the Day of Pentecost, including the manifestation of the Holy Spirit, the gathering of Jews from across the empire, and the preaching of Peter. Theophilus does not know what life in the early Jerusalem church was like or about the powerful deeds performed by the apostles. He must be taught about the church's response to persecution and about how persecution resulted in Samaritans and Gentiles first hearing the message. Luke must even introduce Saul of Tarsus to Theophilus.

Most importantly, Theophilus must learn how the leadership in Jerusalem responded to the influx of Gentiles into the church and how they dealt with the issue of circumcision. He must hear of the establishment of Christian congregations throughout the Roman provinces even in the face of Jewish opposition. And Luke must remind him repeatedly of the innocence of the church, just as he was told of the innocence of Jesus in the Gospel.

So what does the portrait of Luke's imagined reader, Theophilus, look like? Theophilus is an educated, Greek-speaking Gentile familiar with the environs of Rome. He is broadly familiar with the geography of the empire, but he has not traveled to Palestine, Philippi, Thessalonica, or Athens. He speaks Greek, but not Aramaic or Hebrew.

Only presuppositions could lead to the conclusion that Theophilus is a Christian reader. The narratological evidence suggests otherwise. Theophilus is a Gentile "God-fearer," neither a Jew nor a Christian. He knows Judaism from the synagogue and the Scriptures, but in a Hellenistic rather than a Palestinian version. He is familiar with religious experiences of prayer, worship, and a sense of awe in the presence of God. Like many God-fearers, he wishes to be a part of Israel, but he balks at the demands placed on proselytes.

Theophilus has heard Christianity's message, that God is including Gentiles in His purposes. Luke attempts to help this "lover of God" understand the origins and spread of the Christian movement. The narrator apparently hopes, by presenting the stories of people like Theophilus who have responded to the gospel, to persuade him to believe as well.

The Messianic People

The name "Christian" was now being applied to believers in Acts (Acts 11:26). "Christ" is so familiar in its association with Jesus that we practically regard it as His surname. The word, however, is simply the Greek equivalent of "Messiah." Jesus Christ is "Jesus, the Messiah." And "Christian" means "one who belongs to or carries the name of the Messiah." The church is the messianic people of God, continuing the messianic mission Jesus engaged—proclaiming the kingdom of God, bringing healing, good news, forgiveness, new life, and ministry to the people.

As the messianic people of God, we continue the mission of the Suffering Servant, taking up our crosses and following Him. Luke narrates the conception of Jesus, telling how the Holy Spirit came in a human vessel, Mary, to bring the presence of the Messiah into the world. Acts opens with the story of the coming of the Spirit upon human vessels, the apostles and their friends, forming a Spirit-filled community sustaining God's mission. Luke tells of Stephen's trial and death as the first martyr by drawing clear parallels to the trial and death of Jesus Himself. Just as Jesus sets off for Jerusalem in obedience to the will of God in the Gospel, though it would cost Him His life, so does Paul in Acts. The church is the continuing presence of God's messianic mission in the world.

Acts is the story of a new community of Jesus' followers slowly emerging from the cocoon of Judaism and the synagogue. That emergence requires a definition of the essence of the gospel. They must decide what is essential to the message and practice of the life of Jesus. They must determine what is mere cultural husk that can be (must be) discarded as the church moves from

Jerusalem and Judea to the ends of the world. What gospel does a missionary church proclaim when it enters Gentile territory? Acts tells of the church handling the difficult questions of circumcision, law, diet, idolatry, and ethics as it emerges.

Twenty-First Century Church

The 21st century church does not read Acts to learn how to organize or worship. Instead, Acts provides the necessary Voice to remind us who the 21st century church is—the messianic people of God, experiencing life as a community, filled with the Holy Spirit, engaging God's mission in the world. The stories of Acts call the church to sacrifice, obedience, prayer, courage, perseverance, and love.

The Book of Acts teaches the emerging church of the 21st century how to live on mission. In Acts, the church is sent from Jerusalem and Judea to Samaria and the remote parts of the earth. The story is told of the gospel overcoming many obstacles as it makes its way into the Hellenistic world. In the 21st century, the mission field is not limited to foreign cultures in distant places. The church is being sent into the foreign culture that surrounds it, which is the modern world. In the passing shadow of modernity, the church emerges into an encounter with an entirely different culture.

The movement from the culture of modernity to the culture of postmodernity requires the church to think intentionally and strategically about what is happening, just as taking the gospel into a foreign society requires analysis of culture and a learning of language and customs. The church transforms itself by engaging the mission.

The Essential Gospel

Consequently, Acts suggests a model for contemporary efforts to emerge from the thoughts, practices, and culture of modernity into a very different world. The church's challenge now is to send missionaries, not simply into another country, but into another century. This, too, requires serious missiological reflection. The essential gospel needs to be defined. The story of Jesus and His community needs to be retold in a way that it can be understood by the very people the church hopes to include in future chapters of the story of God and His people.

Understanding Acts

by Greg Garrett, Tim Keel, and Chuck Smith, Jr.

The Second Installment

It is generally known that in duplicating a video the second tape will lose a generation. To "lose a generation" means that a copy of an original analog tape is inferior because the quality of the sound and images of the second generation is diminished in the duplication process. As in video duplication, the main characters in Acts cannot come close to the presence of Jesus with His charisma and dynamic personality found in the Gospels. How could they? He was the Son of God! All they have is His name, which they use as if it were their power of attorney in Jesus' absence (for example, Acts 3:6-8,15-16; 4:8-12,18).

But what was true of the older analog tapes is not true of newer digital recordings. Digital copies do not lose a generation, and neither does Acts. Acts reveals the presence and activity of Jesus Christ through the life of His church and its leaders as clearly as the Gospels reveal His activities on earth.

The Book of Acts is the second installment of Luke's two-volume work. Together, the Gospel of Luke (the longest book in the New Testament) and Acts (slightly shorter than Luke) make up one-quarter of the New Testament. The first step in developing a well-informed understanding of Acts is to read it through the lens of Luke's Gospel. In other words, think of Acts as "Part 2" in the story of Jesus. In Part 1, Luke "recounted the events of Jesus' life—His actions, His teachings from the beginning of His life until He was taken up into heaven" (Acts 1:1-2). Part 2 reports the ongoing ministry of Jesus "after He entered heaven and took His place at God's right hand" (Acts 2:33; 7:56). In Acts, Jesus is still at the heart of God's new work on earth; He continues to heal (Acts 4:9-10), to confront His persecutors (Acts 9:3-6), and to direct the ministries of His apostles (for example, Acts 16:7; 22:10-21). The gospel that spreads throughout the world is the message of Jesus Christ.

Two Eyewitness Accounts

If we place Luke and Acts in sequence, the narrative that begins in the temple in Jerusalem (Luke 1:5-9), the heart of the Jewish faith, concludes under house arrest in Rome (Acts 28:16,30-31), the heart of the Gentile nations. Luke and Acts both reveal Luke's interest in the eyewitness accounts of the events he narrates. Once Jesus explained that His disciples would be His witnesses, Luke built this theme into the structure of the story (Acts 2:32; 3:15; 5:32 among others). A quick survey of these references reveals that the truth to which the apostles witnessed was that Jesus Christ was alive, working miracles, and opening the door to the kingdom of God for all humanity. For this reason, Luke stresses from the very beginning that Jesus "showed His apostles that He was alive—appearing to them repeatedly over a period of 40 days, giving them many convincing proofs of His resurrection" (Acts 1:2-3).

When Will You Establish Your Kingdom?

The story of Acts opens with Jesus and His disciples, who now realize their time with the Lord is winding down. Given the nature of these last moments together, they ask Jesus the question that burned in their hearts, "Is now the time, Lord— the time when You will reestablish Your kingdom in our land of Israel?" (Acts 1:6). Jesus refused to divulge God's calendar; instead, He explained to them what would immediately follow His departure. His instructions prepared them for a mission that would occupy them in the days and years ahead.

Although the teaching of the kingdom of God does not have as great a role in Acts as it did in Matthew, Mark, and Luke, it is nevertheless an important theme that forms a bracket for the entire Book of Acts. The nature of God's kingdom as Jesus presented it in Luke (e.g., "the kingdom of God is already here among you," Luke 17:21) was the miracle of God's reign breaking into human history in His own life and ministry (Luke 10:8-9,11). Even if the Kingdom had not yet arrived in its nation-shattering fullness and was hidden from most people (Luke 8:10), still the Father had chosen gladly to give the Kingdom to Jesus' disciples (Luke 12:32).

The disciples were laboring under a previous paradigm of God's kingdom, until Paul's ministry (Acts 14:22). At the end of the book (Acts 28:31), Luke makes a strong association between three braided themes of spiritual power: the Kingdom, the Spirit, and the name of Jesus.

The apostles' question regarding the Kingdom provoked Jesus to articulate the theme (perhaps even a table of contents) for the Book of Acts. He told them, "You will receive power when the Holy Spirit comes on you. And you will be My witnesses, first here in Jerusalem, then beyond to Judea and Samaria, and finally to the farthest places on earth" (Acts 1:8). The apostles would be supernaturally empowered as witnesses to Jesus. To what were they to "give witness"? Probably the entire Gospel of Luke, "from His ceremonial washing by John until His ascension" (Acts 1:22). They would stress the facts that the Jesus they knew was God's Messiah, that His death served the purpose of God by providing forgiveness for sins (Acts 3:19), that Jesus rose from the dead (Acts 2:23-24,32-33; 3:14-15), and that through the name of Jesus Christ, God was now accessible to "everyone who calls on the name of the Lord" (Acts 2:21).

The Promise of the Father

The Gospel of Luke ends with an ellipsis, an unfulfilled promise. The disciples saw with their own eyes the fulfillment of Old Testament prophecies regarding Israel's Messiah and "witnessed the fulfillment of these things." But first they needed to receive "My Father's promise to you . . . power from heaven" (Luke 24:46-49). That is roughly where the Gospel of Luke concludes, leaving his readers in suspense as to what happened next. Acts begins exactly where Luke left off, taking up the somewhat cryptic phrase, "the promise of the Father" (Acts 1:4).

If Luke connects Acts to his first volume on the life of Jesus, then he is equally concerned to connect the narrative of both volumes to the bigger story of the Old Testament. In the first episode of Acts after the ascension of Jesus, the disciples turned to the Old Testament Scriptures to define and interpret their circumstances and to find guidance for their next step (Acts 1:15-17). Luke had made these Old Testament connections throughout his Gospel (see especially Luke 24:25-27, 44-45), and the apostle will continue to do so throughout the Book of Acts. Also, Stephen's defense in Acts 7 will be a typically Old Testament recitation of Israel's history leading up to its rejection of Jesus Christ.

The fulfillment and theology of Scripture is only one way that Luke makes use of the Old Testament. In a manner that is unique to Luke's Gospel, the supernatural experience of Israel's charismatic leaders continues on in the lives of New Testament characters. For example, John the Baptist was "filled with the Spirit" even prior to his birth, and so were his mother, Elizabeth, and father, Zacharias (Luke 1:15, 42, 67). Perhaps even more dramatically, the Spirit, who descended on Jesus at His baptism, filled Him and then led Him around in the wilderness for 40 days (Luke 4:1,14). Afterward Jesus returned to Galilee in the "power of the Spirit" before returning to Nazareth. In the synagogue in Nazareth, He took the scroll of Isaiah, read the reference, and then announced, "The Spirit of the Lord is upon Me" (Luke 3:22; 4:1,14,17-18).

Moses and the Prophets

To appreciate these references, we need to rewind to Israel's encampment in the wilderness when Moses wished that God would put His Spirit upon all His people so they all would prophesy (Numbers 11:29). If everyone in the Old Testament did not experience this divine energizing, then who did receive it? In the Old Testament, the Spirit came upon judges, kings, prophets, and military leaders" (for example, Judges 6:34). Jesus described this in a similar way when He told His disciples the power of God would come upon them. In other words, in the Old Testament the Spirit of God filled special people to fulfill a special mission.

Almost as if responding to Moses' wish, the prophet Joel announced a day when God would pour out His Spirit on all humanity so that even children would be prophesying (Joel 2:28). We need to be aware of this prediction because this is what John the Baptist had in mind when he said the followers of Jesus would be "washed with the Holy Spirit," and it is what the Lord had in mind when He said, "You will receive power when the Holy Spirit comes on you" (Acts 1:5, 8). The dramatic fulfillment of this long-expected blessing occurs in Acts 2, a fulfillment that was not lost on Peter who stood up and announced, "This is about the fulfillment of the prophecy of Joel" (Acts 2:16).

As the story unfolds, Luke explores the extent of Joel's prophecy and fulfillment. He takes special interest in the work of the Holy Spirit in the lives of ordinary men and women, including Samaritans and Gentiles (Acts 6:5; 8:14-17; 10:44-46).

Threats to the Community of Believers

Acts 1:14 beautifully depicts in seed-form the community of believers that forms around the person and mission of Jesus Christ. They are, in fact, a spiritual community that listens to the Scriptures and the Holy Spirit (Acts 1:16). For the rest of the story, the healthy church operates as a loving society of believers in Jesus Christ whose members learn to apply charismatic and biblical solutions to practical problems.

The "oneness" they enjoy in that first meeting, however, is threatened throughout the narrative, first by institutional religion, second by Christian believers who still have loyalties to Judaism (Acts 15:5), and finally by Gentile rulers. This tension in Acts moves the plot forward—a tension Jesus alluded to in the metaphor of new wine and old wineskins (Luke 5:33-39).

What they leave behind for us is the example of a dynamic community life illuminated by Scripture and the Spirit, which together reveal the way to the next horizon.

In the Name of Jesus

There are only a few references to Jesus' name in Acts. We see that in the hearts and mouths of the apostles His name was accompanied by power. In fact, this was the reason Jesus gave His followers the use of His name. Jesus was certainly present when Peter took the crippled man by the hand at the temple gate and said, "Stand up and walk in the name of Jesus of Nazareth, the Liberating King" (Acts 3:6). Through the use of the name, the presence of Jesus was constantly brought into immediate contact with humans who needed salvation, healing, or exorcism. This is what it means to "invoke the name of Jesus."

Of all the lessons we learn in Acts regarding living with the vital presence of Jesus in our world today, none may be more important than learning to invite Him into our homes, our circumstances, the dark parts of our souls, or the farthest reaches of the earth. Call Him into your feelings. Do this, and Jesus will enter and redeem your experience. If you keep the two separate—Jesus and your emotions—then you lose whatever lesson He may have taught through your feelings and thoughts. Without calling on Jesus' name, your focus is on yourself rather than on His direction and healing.

Peter the Man of Passion

Peter is a passionate man given to rash decisions and bold declarations. Perhaps his decision to heed Jesus' invitation to discipleship is such a choice. Abandoning a fishing trade that was likely passed down from one generation to the next could not have been easy. But he did it. And so we might assume that alongside Peter's passionate, rash, and bold personality is a man who lives instinctively. Thus, the biblical portrait of Peter is not simply that of a man making bold declarations, but of a man struggling to live those things he has pronounced. Peter sees and says things in the moment that have profound implications and require intense transformation.

In Peter, we see a man exposed: all his glory, all his faults. He is not like those enigmatic characters in the Bible, inscrutable people who come and go shrouded in mystery. Not the apostle Peter! While mysterious characters like Enoch appear briefly in the pages of Scripture and disappear to "be with God" in transcendent holy moments, we watch Peter struggle and scrape along his way, trying to keep up with a Lord and Savior who seems intent on defying every expectation a religious and righteous Jew might have. Peter is very human.

Peter lived by his gut, and it tells him something about Jesus. In fact, his gut tells him all kinds of things, especially when he is around Jesus. In the heat of the moment, Peter is presumably led by the Holy Spirit, and his instincts tell him something. He can't help himself. He speaks. When Jesus asks His disciples to guess about the nature of His identity, Peter blurts out, "You are the Messiah!" Other times he seems less than inspired. When Peter accompanies Jesus onto the mount of transfiguration and sees Him transformed and joined by Moses and Elijah, we hear him stutter, "Let's build a shelter." When Jesus, on the eve of His death, warns the disciples about the coming trial, Peter objects, "I'm going all the way to the end with You" (Luke 22:33). There are many others: rebuking Jesus for teaching that the Messiah must suffer, stating, "You will not wash my feet!" then deciding, "Don't stop with my feet. Cleanse my hands and head as well!" (John 13:8-9). In Peter we see a man captivated and perplexed by Jesus. He sees something in the moment, and he can't help but declare it. At the same time, declaring something doesn't mean necessarily knowing or believing the declaration.

Peter the Shepherd

Because Peter is a leader, he must also shepherd others along the same path. This is what is happening in the second chapter of Acts. The Holy Spirit of God descends upon the embryonic, emerging church worshiping in Jerusalem on Pentecost. They begin to speak in foreign languages proclaiming the power of God's saving deeds. Those who surround them have no explanation for this, so like the priest Eli did before them, they interpret Spirit-generated activity as public drunkenness. What is a guy like Peter to do in such a case? What else? Speak!

To the Jews gathered in Jerusalem, Peter declares the fulfillment of Joel's prophecy of the final days through the revelation of God's Messiah, Jesus Christ. Peter tells of His ministry, His death by betrayal, and His ultimate vindication by God through resurrection. He goes further, extending to these Jews the same invitation that he himself received from the Lord he now proclaims. Finally, he declares that God's life and kingdom are accessible to those previously excluded, namely the Gentiles. The implications of what God accomplished in Christ relating to Jews and Gentiles was an issue the early church wrestled with for a long time.

Peter the Rock

Do you wonder if Peter would have been better off staying quiet? The proverbs describe at length the wisdom of silence. When you are quiet, you at least have the appearance of wisdom. But I'm not so sure we always need that particular kind of wisdom. Jesus didn't seem to think so. Remember, we have a record of Jesus personally isolating Peter and telling him that he is the rock upon whom He will build His church. Maybe the church needs leaders like Peter at times of upheaval and transition, leaders who have had an encounter with the Messiah and know deep in their souls that everything has changed. Even if they don't know how to reckon the change or what it will mean, they have experienced something that moves them to speak boldly, even if it takes time for their own lives and the church to catch up.

True Church, Real Community

The early church we read about in Acts was not a product of culture—it was countercultural. The individual churches were characterized by their locations—the gatherings described in Acts on Solomon's Porch were clearly composed largely of Jews (who saw God coming to them in a new way), while the individual churches who received letters from Paul each had their own particular challenges, gifts, and social settings—although they were called to something higher and above any individual identity. Something that was above any national or cultural identity.

Like the Hebrews who were carried off to Babylon 600 years before the birth of Christ, believers are called to be faithful to God in a land that is hostile to many of the values of God. (This is not an anti-national sentiment for any country, but it is an observation about our culture. In a time when the poor are neglected, starving, and even left to die of curable diseases, the rich build bigger houses and buy bigger vehicles, and everyone in our society tries to emulate them.) We are called to care less about things and more about people, even if that makes us as resident aliens in the place we have called home. Instead of trying to glorify ourselves, as Ananias and Sapphira do, we are called to be countercultural—to give ourselves to God without reservation, along with our gifts, our time, and our money. Those are startling words, but Acts shows us how the early church lived them.

From its beginnings, the church has been truest to its purpose when it welcomes others into a community that feels like home—growing out of specific cultural needs and history—and when it pushes to rise above any parts of their society that don't fit the story of God. The church likewise may be truest to its purposes when individual congregations form as communities, with specific gifts and challenges, and when it seeks to renew society, by speaking in a prophetic voice to the culture—even if, like the church in Acts, it has to speak in the words and images of that culture to be understood.

Power in the Name

Peter and John confront those standing in Solomon's Porch after they healed a lame man who had spent much of his life begging there (Acts 3:1-11). In response to the crowd's question, "Who gave you the authority to create that spectacle in the temple yesterday?" (Acts 4:7), Peter answers that they've performed this miracle in the name of Jesus of Nazareth, who was God's Liberator but whom the people killed in accordance with God's plan. Peter and John confront these people—and the leaders of the Jews who imprisoned them—not only with the fact of Jesus' power, but also with their complicity in Jesus' death.

Some Christians have sought power—political power, at least—and have been willing to be incredibly confrontational, both about elements of secular society and with other people of faith who disagree with them. Other Christians, in an attempt to seem reasonable or to distance themselves from some of the more controversial stands taken by the first group, have been leery of power and confrontation. But these passages from Acts are clear—we are called to power, although the power to change lives and to mend the world comes from God, through Jesus, not from the hands or minds or organization of the disciples. Peter tells the onlookers, "This man standing in front of you . . . was healed by the authority of Jesus" (Acts 4:10).

Doing What Is Right

When brought before the council and ordered to stop teaching and healing in the name of Jesus, the disciples don't try to take control, even though the council fears the huge number of people who have already been persuaded to follow Jesus. History tells us that religion is almost always truer to its foundational beliefs and stronger in its faith when it opposes a culture instead of supporting it. Peter and John don't threaten the council with their authority to teach and heal; they gently but firmly tell them, "You are the judges here, so we'll leave it up to you to judge whether it is right in the sight of God to obey your commands or God's. *But one thing we can tell you:* we cannot possibly restrain ourselves from speaking about what we have seen and heard with our own eyes and ears" (Acts 4:19-20).

We could restate Psalm 137:4, "Such cruel men taunted us—haunted our memories. How could we not sing, while still tormented, brokenhearted, homesick? Please don't make us sing this song." To do what is right in the eyes of the Lord is more important than obeying customs or man-made laws. To obey God is more important than obeying human beings. And if the dictates of God and of society come into conflict, then Acts shows us that Christians have a duty to stand with God and against culture. For churches today, that might mean objecting to war as a problem-solving mechanism; it might mean opposing a society that highly values consumerism; it might mean calling for economic sanctions against a nation practicing genocide. Individual churches have championed all of these causes. Each community of faith might interpret God's word to them in a different way, but faithfulness, at its core, means a commitment to justice, peace, and courageous belief in Jesus—regardless of what the culture, or even other elements of the church, might say in response.

Connecting to the Culture

But we don't have to insult people who believe differently—even if we want to. The gentleness and confidence Peter and John exhibit when they are asked to stand before powerful people is remarkable. They tell hard truths, but they treat the authorities with respect, couching their arguments in an appeal to wisdom and discernment.

In other words, they speak the Sanhedrin language, even if they don't necessarily accept all its conclusions. Peter and John talk with the people in Solomon's Porch and the authorities within that gathering as people with a shared language, history, and culture. Peter describes Jesus as God's Liberator in their common language of prophets, faith, and understanding. In a later section of Acts, the apostle Paul speaks in Athens to the Stoic and Epicurean philosophers in a language and reasoning they can understand, according to their own beliefs. He even quotes a line from a Greek poet they would have known, saying it has become a significant statement of Christian belief despite its pagan origins: "We live in God; we move in God; we exist in God" (Acts 17:28).

It's here that churches in tune to contemporary culture have strongly connected—and must continue connecting—to the example of the early church. Through references to music, movies, and other elements of our shared culture, our writers, teachers, and preachers in the connected church have done as the leaders in Acts did. They respectfully but firmly have taught how ideas, characters, and themes we find in contemporary culture—in music or movies—can illuminate parts of the Christian story in a new and powerful way. A potent recent example out of such teaching is the similarity between the *Matrix* story and the story of God's Redeemer, Jesus. In a day when miracles seem to be more about recognition than about the action itself, this may be the greatest way for us to connect with others about the good news of Jesus the Redeemer.

Trying to Control God

The miracles we see recorded in these passages from Acts—the healing of the crippled man and the miraculous escape from prison—are evidence of the power of God working on behalf of John and Peter. Because they believed in the power of the name of Jesus, they could call upon His name (Acts 3:6), and Jesus' name gave them the power to do His healing and liberating work.

Do we see these kinds of miracles today? We may—we can all think of people who have prayed for deliverance, healing, or reconciliation, and they have received what they sought. The question we often have, though, is what we do when prayers seem to go unanswered—or to be answered in the negative. Faith-filled people throughout history have been killed and tortured, have died of cancer or in car wrecks, or have prayed for the deliverance of others that never came. Is it because of superior faith that one is healed, or because of sin that one has an ailment? Neither. Jesus says such trials allow God to reveal Himself (John 9:3). Trying to gauge our faithfulness by whether we are able to turn God's power to our purposes is futile—we must pray for God's will, even though our own wishes are powerful. God can't be controlled as a sorcerer controls magic. We are to pray for God's will to be accomplished (1 John 5:14). If God chooses to heal and restore someone, as Peter's prayer restored the lame man, then let us rejoice. And if God chooses not to heal the lame man or chooses to leave us in a prison we've been thrown into for following Him, then let us rejoice still.

The Pharisee Gamaliel counsels his fellow authorities wisely, "If this is just another movement arising from human enthusiasm, it will die out soon enough. But then again, if God is in this, you won't be able to stop it—unless, of course, you're ready to fight against God!" (Acts 5:38-39).

Two millennia later, it is clear that this movement was inspired by God and has many lessons to teach us. May it continue to be inspired by God, and may we always seek that inspiration.

THE ELBOW OF ACTS

by Andrew Jones

Radical Upheaval

The apostle Peter in Antioch witnessed the radical upheaval in the early church. More significant than ours, yet not dissimilar. The major shift involving the inclusion of the Samaritans and Gentiles in the mission of God is a dominant theme in Luke's writing, hinted at in the Gospel of Luke and then highlighted in his account of the Acts of the Apostles. In fact, a reading of both volumes is essential for watching the full story unravel. This emphasis of Luke's Gospel for all the nations is announced by Jesus (Luke 4) and is inherent in His commission to the disciples (Luke 24:47). More than the other Gospel writers, Luke gives special attention to Jesus' dealings with Samaritans and Gentiles, in particular His meals with "sinners," and their equivalents in Acts such as the meal table of Cornelius (Acts 10). The geographical expansion is staged at the beginning of Acts (Acts 1:8) and its progression tracked all the way to Rome.

The Hinge of the Elbow

If Acts is a record of the early church in transition, then chapters 10—13 are the elbow joint, the hinge, the point of departure from the known, and the start of a strange and exciting pilgrimage to the corners of the world. In just four short chapters, we see a shift from a predominantly Jewish church centered in Jerusalem to an increasingly international church based in Antioch. The optimistic tone of the church had been dampened through the unexpectedly delayed return of Christ, and persecution was driving the relocation of believers into new and strange cities. We enter these chapters with Peter and leave with Paul as the central figurehead leading the expansion north into non-Jewish territory.

A fantastic example of this is the account of Peter and Cornelius in Acts 10. Cornelius, like Lydia and the Philippian jailer, is one of those "people of peace" (Luke 10). God contacts him long before Peter hears of it. God initiates. Both men hear God speak to them. Cornelius sends three men to Peter, and Peter arrives with double that number. In Cornelius's house, the number increases again to include his household (*oikos*). A community has been formed. They eat together, Jew and Gentile. Peter preaches and is himself converted to a new understanding of God. Cornelius receives a gift and gives a gift back. This is dialogue more than monologue. Pilgrimage more than patronage. How very different from the model of missions I grew up with and often participated in.

The gospel is now embraced and passed on by Gentiles through new complex social networks such as the world had never seen. The rapid spread of the good news of Jesus to "the ends of the earth" (Acts 13:47) would take advantage of a common language, strategic centers (Roland Allen), safe Roman roads, and existing social networks.

Paul's Journeys

In his excellent book on complexity and networks,[5] Albert–Laszlo Barabasi introduces his world of scale free networks with two historical examples: The teenage hacker, known as Mafia Boy, and the apostle Paul, who "was a master of first-century social and religious links, the only network at the beginning of the modern era that could carry and spread a faith."

While Barabasi's observation on complex networks is astute and quite relevant to the scale free growth of online Christian communities and portals today, his focus on Paul's strategy as the primary reason for Christianity's success is only part of the picture. As Luke records the beginning of Paul's journeys in these chapters, he makes it clear that Paul, Peter, Barnabas, Silas, and the other missionaries are following their Lord's commands and example. Their strategy is largely given to them through prayer, visions, dreams, and prophecies. God guides them and hinders them, sends them out and brings them back. They use their abilities, yes, but they are on God's mission. The reception or rejection of their message is a litmus test of whether they should stay or move on. And moving on is signaled by the wiping of dust from their feet.

Once in Antioch Pisidia (Acts 13), a small coastal town, the message of Christ to the whole city was rejected by the Jewish authorities. Paul and Barnabas together responded with great confidence: "OK, then. It was only right that we should bring God's message to you Jewish people first. But now, since you are rejecting our message and identifying yourselves as unworthy of eternal

---

5 Albert-Laszlo Barabasi, *Linked: How Everything Is Connected to Everything Else and What It Means for Business, Science and Everyday Life* (London: Penguin, 2003).

life, we are now turning to the Gentiles." Jesus had made it clear that the good news should be offered to the Jewish nation first, and after that, the non-Jewish. The strategic instructions Jesus gives to the twelve (Luke 9) and also to the larger group (Luke 10) find their fractal echo through the Acts of the Apostles. They are continuing the mission of Jesus and doing it His way—locating people and places of peace, finding favorable environments for the reception of God's gift. If that favor is not there, they are told to wipe the dust off their feet and move on:

> [50]But the Jewish leaders united the aristocratic religious women and the city's leading men in opposition to Paul and Barnabas, and soon they were being persecuted and were driven out of their territory. [51]They simply shook the dust off their feet in protest and moved on to Iconium. [52]The disciples weren't intimidated at all, but rather were full of joy and the Holy Spirit." (Acts 13:50-52)

A Bit About Feet And Heels

Feet have always been ugly things to me: smelly, dirty, and only worthy to live inside shoes. But the feet of God's messengers are described differently in the Scriptures:

> How beautiful on the mountains are the feet of those who bring good news of peace and salvation (Isaiah 52:7).

Feet carry the gift over barriers and through gateways to find joyful reception. Jesus washed the feet of His disciples. He was preparing obedient apostolic feet for their beautiful task. But there was one disciple who refused to offer his foot—Judas—who "lifted up his heel" at Jesus. A heel turned away is one that cannot be washed. It is unsuitable. It refuses beauty. Disobedient, it follows another path.

The foot washing changed the makeup of the group. The team of twelve disciples was now a divided group comprising eleven Feet and one Heel. It was aggregated by Jesus now as directional rather than categorical, "centered" rather than "bounded," grouped by their common commitment to the ideological center rather than delineated by the boundary line of "Member" or "Non-Member."

Hirsch and Frost find these concepts of "bounded" and "centered" (taken from missiologist Paul Hiebert) instrumental in describing ministry in the emerging-missional church. It is the understanding of the centered set rather than the bounded set ("wells" rather than "fences"),[6] which allows for massive diversity and for a deeper underlying unity based on Jesus. This is also helpful in understanding the rejection of the Jews that preceded the mission to the Gentiles. The Jewish nation (a culturally bounded set) has rejected the gospel of Jesus, but the Jews (an ideologically centered set) have become divided between those who have rejected and those who have received the good news of Jesus. Luke makes it clear, in this passage and in those that follow, that wherever there is rejection, there are also Jews who receive the message gladly and become followers of Jesus.

At the foot washing, Jesus said to Peter, "If I do not wash you, you have no part with Me" (John 13:8). To share in the life and mission of Jesus is to represent Him as ambassadors. "Whoever accepts the One I send, accepts Me, and whoever accepts Me accepts the One who sent Me" (John 13:20). Perhaps this is another kind of grouping: A "distributed" set, aggregated by those who partake in the mission of Christ and those who refuse.

---

6 Michael Frost and Alan Hirsch, *The Shaping of Things to Come, Innovation and Mission for the 21st Century.* (Peabody, MA: Hendrickson, 2003), 209.

Paul's Mission to the Gentiles

by David Capes

Paul's Example

By all accounts, Saul the Pharisee, the former persecutor of the church, is credited as the one who engineered and established the mission to the nations. More than any other, he dislodged "the Way" from its cultural and territorial moorings so that it could reach the ends of the earth, just as Isaiah had predicted. Luke's insistence that believers remember Paul's example is more than an interesting feature of Luke's story. It's a central theme. In other words, Luke wants us to learn from Paul how our congregations can extend the mission of the Liberating King into our changing culture.

Everything Paul did was intentional, strategic. We see his strategies on every page of Luke's Acts. Often, today's church leaders look to mega-churches to see what they are doing and which programs are working. Then we try to duplicate those programs or methods in our own fields. Results are frequently mixed. Watching the strategies of the mega-churches can provide us some help, but they're not the only places where we ought to seek guidance. Rather than looking to modern trends, Luke invites us to learn from the Apostle to the Gentiles, then to return to our times and situations with a renewed sense of what the church is and how we ought to tactically approach our own mission.

Urban Strategy

Paul's mission strategy took him first to the cities. This was appropriate for two reasons. First, Paul himself was a city-fellow, and Paul knew he would be most effective with people like himself. Some call this the "homogenous unit principle." Rather than retreat in embarrassment from this principle of social behavior, we ought to accept it and then exploit it. This doesn't mean, of course, that we shouldn't try to transcend the limitations of our unique "flocks." If we want to be effective in our own mission strategies, then we have to know who we are. But there is second reason that Paul's mission strategy was primarily urban: he went to where the people gathered. They might live outside the city, but weekly they would journey to the city to shop, trade, and worship in the synagogues and temples lining the main roads of these Roman cities. Paul's strategy is clear: we must go to where most of the people are.

Two Heads—Better than One

Paul was a man of his time, not of ours. In Paul's day, there were no rugged individualists, no self-made men. He knew well what modern generations have forgotten: humans are hard-wired for community. He knew the mission would be most effective with the vitality, support, protection, help, and wisdom of a community of like-minded, otherwise-gifted men and women deeply committed to "the Way." Paul taught that the church was a body, not a business. In this body, members are organically connected, mutually dependent, and spiritually animated. The church is a family, a household of faith, with God as Father, Jesus as elder brother, and fellow believers as brothers and sisters. If we gain anything from a gentle read through Acts, we will lose the business mentality and embrace a more organic, human, team approach to kingdom work.

Cross-cultural Mission

Paul was no fool. He didn't enter a city and immediately look up the local atheists and skeptics. His strategy took him to communities and places where people already believed in God, knew the Scriptures, and shared similar perspectives on the world. He went to the Jews first. Whenever Paul entered a city, he looked first for the local synagogue. Paul did this not only because it made sense. He did it because the prophecies had to be fulfilled. To Paul's profound sorrow, often Jews in the cities he visited rejected both the gospel and Paul himself. He worshiped with them, shared with them, argued the meaning of Scripture with them, and sometimes ran from their stones. When the opposition became stiff—or should we say hard as a rock—Paul shook the dust off his feet in symbolic protest and took the message of Jesus to the God-fearing Gentiles (those non-Jews who were attracted to the one God of Israel and closely identified, without losing their skins, with the Jews). We don't know the depth of his discomfort the first time he ate a meal prepared by one who didn't follow the purity rituals.

We didn't invent cross-cultural missions. It started in Antioch and Galatia, around a common table, as Jews and Gentiles broke bread together. There is something unique about table fellowship. For us the table means friendship. It is an overture to enter with us in a relationship that is risky, open, and transparent. To be "on mission" means we sit often at the table with new friends, we open up our lives, and we bear witness. It means that we learn of other cultures, eat strange foods, and stop insisting that everybody be like us. Like Paul we may start our mission by sharing Christ with people who look, talk, and act like we do, but we had better not stop there. One day we will sit at the table with people gathered from the four corners of the world, representing every family, every tribe, and every nation. A good deal of ministry happens "in church" around liturgies, especially as we break the bread and drink the wine of the Eucharist. But the spiritual power of the Eucharist is ultimately found in the love feast and in dinners at our homes, with people like and unlike us.

Found—Common Ground

When Paul began his ministry in a city, whether with Jews or Gentiles, he worked hard to find common ground. In the synagogue, marketplace, and homes that welcomed him, Paul preached Christ after connecting with his audiences. Generally speaking, when Paul stood with the Jews, he found common ground in the Scriptures, their common heritage, and shared history. As he read and reread his Bible, Paul saw the story of Jesus in the characters, plots, hopes, and warnings of the scrolls. Today, the entire Bible, both Old and New Testaments, forms a vital backdrop to our culture and lives. In our Western culture, there is a residue of the Christian story. Who hasn't met a "Good Samaritan" or heard "the Golden Rule"? This residue offers us a location where we can move deeper with our friends and fellow citizens into the Scriptures. If we are open to these kinds of conversations, we will find ample opportunities to share our unique stories.

Too often, Christians today avoid music, movies, and literature that are not immersed in obvious Christian themes. When we isolate ourselves in this way, we cut ourselves off from a great source of inspiration and truth. Art, music, literature, and movies are all created by people made in the image of God. Even if the divine image has suffered under the domination of sin, "secular" art betrays what it means to be human. We see in secular forms the beauty of creation, the ugliness of sin, and the need for redemption, meaning, and life. We should recognize secular art for what it is: attempts to capture and express truth in a world longing for reconciliation. When we study a culture respectfully, we will find in every expression an opportunity to bear witness to the broader, deeper truth recognized by the church, that part of the world already reconciled to God through Christ.

Preached the *Kerygma*

Paul laid a foundation with a simple message, the *kerygma*. *Kerygma* is a Greek term, meaning "preaching" or "proclamation." It does not refer to the style (how) or location (where) of the preaching. It refers to the content of the gospel. In short, Paul's *kerygma* consisted of these essential points:

1. Jesus inaugurated the fulfillment of messianic prophecy.
2. He did good and performed miracles.
3. He was crucified according to God's plan.
4. He was resurrected and exalted to the right hand of God the Father.
5. He will come again in glory, honor, and judgment.
6. Therefore, repent, believe, and be baptized.

When he was permitted, Paul declared this gospel message among Jews and Gentiles. The message was simple, but powerful. God has acted decisively in and through Jesus, who is the long-awaited Messiah or Liberating King. In Jesus God has come to us and acted in history for all to see. At the heart of the message is a crucified Messiah, vindicated in the resurrection. For Paul, Christ had changed everything; a new creation had begun. The *parousia* (second coming) of Jesus would complete what He started. Because all this is true, the only proper response is for men and women, Jew and Gentile, slave and free, to change how they think and act, put faith in Christ, and undergo baptism (ceremonial washing) in His name.

Spent Time

When Paul was on his mission, he didn't pop in for brief appearances only to pop out the next day at dawn. He spent time with people, living with them in the cities he targeted for mission. On occasion, he stayed for months or years in the same place. On mission, he accepted their hospitality, ate their bread, slept in their homes, and shared the gospel. He lived life and journeyed with his people. He knew the gospel was too important to just drop in for a short visit.

This part of Paul's mission strategy is challenging to apply in our day when travel is easy. We are often discouraged, ready to shake the dust off our feet and move to greener pastures. Of course, short-term mission opportunities are not without value. When it comes to beginning new churches, however, the only strategy that works is spending time in a particular place with a particular people. It means preaching the gospel and living the gospel in full view of everyone.

Appointed Leaders

When it was time for Paul to move on to the next city, he appointed leaders to guide the fledgling community until he or an apprentice could return. He looked for people whose giftedness by the Spirit was obvious. His letters demonstrate how he would match duties with gifts. But Paul insisted that every gift was for the common good, not for individual enjoyment or power. He believed every member of Christ's body had a gift, and every gift was important.

The need for leaders has never been greater than it is today. We must work diligently to match duties with gifts. Discerning gifts is not as tricky as some have made it. We don't need a spiritual gift inventory to figure out what gifts we or someone else has. Rather, it is a matter of knowing members of the congregation well and recognizing when the grace of God is present in their service. We need to be in tune to the working of the Spirit of God to see His gifts at work in the midst of our churches.

Prayed for His Churches

In Acts and in all his letters, we read that Paul constantly prayed for the individual churches. This may seem obvious, but it is amazing how much work and how little prayer go into our missions. For Paul prayer was not just a nice thing to do when time allowed; it was a strategic part of his work. A study of Paul's prayers for his churches is revealing. How a person prays and what a person prays reveals much about his or her understanding of the mission. As Paul prayed for his churches, he grew in love, compassion, respect, and grace toward those he called his spiritual children, his brothers and sisters.

Revisited When He Could

A close reading of Acts and Paul's letters demonstrates another important aspect of Paul's missionary strategy. Whenever possible, the apostle returned to the churches he founded for encouragement, correction, and support. These benefits could go both ways; that is the nature of reciprocal living within the body of Christ. The Christian life is life together, a shared journey, a common purpose and destiny. One of the key phrases we see in Paul's writings is "one another." Constantly Paul exhorts his followers to walk in his paths and "greet one another," "love one another," "forgive one another," "encourage one another," and so on. Paul knew that the Christian life could not be lived alone; it had to be lived in relation to "one another." But Paul also knew that his churches continued to need his wisdom, passion, and spirit if they were to be successful.

Sent Delegates

There were times when Paul couldn't return to a church he founded because he was either in prison or he was involved in another ministry. So when he couldn't visit himself, he sent his coworkers as his representatives. These were not short-term associates, interns, or someone conveniently available. These were people who had walked with Paul through thick and thin. These were men Paul could trust. When his delegates arrived and stood before the community, they spoke for Paul and acted as his hands and feet in the church until Paul could be present again with them.

Wrote Letters

Although Acts never mentions it, Paul was a prolific letter writer. We don't know how many letters he wrote to churches and individuals, but the New Testament contains 13 letters under his name. He likely wrote many more. When Paul couldn't revisit a church or when he didn't have a designated delegate to send, Paul wrote a letter. His letters were a substitute for his presence. Paul's letters were not like our random email or quick phone calls; his letters were literary events. They took a long time and a lot of material resources (in our economy that would mean hundreds of dollars) to produce and send to his churches. Paul's letters were collaborative efforts with coworkers, secretaries, and patrons. The courier who carried his letter not only delivered it, but read it to the gathered church. (Remember, not everyone could read or read well enough in front of a crowd.) It was the courier's task to interpret Paul's mood or teaching. In the end, Paul's letters have become his lasting legacy.

Connect the Churches

When Paul preached the crucified Christ, those he baptized knew they were becoming a part of something greater than their local community. Through faith they were entering into God's covenant with the patriarch Abraham, a covenant of promise for a world-wide blessing. In this sense, Paul connected his churches to the past. But Paul also connected his churches to the present faith-in-Christ communities that dotted the landscapes of Judea, Galilee, Syria, Asia, and Greece. Paul's churches shared leadership, financial concerns (for example, the relief offering for Jerusalem), and a common purpose/theology. They sang the same hymns, read the same Scripture, spoke the same confessions, and practiced the same sacraments (baptism and the Lord's table). They were collectively the body of Christ, locally present in their various cities.

Today, denominational loyalties are on the decline. Because of this, contemporary churches can become more disconnected and isolated than in the past. Denominationalism, despite its dangers, has the advantage of linking churches to something outside themselves. With great affluence and impressive size some churches decide to go it alone, acting as if they don't need anything outside themselves. Like an island to themselves, whatever they need, they grow (literature, leadership, missions, financial resources, and so on). At the same time, there is a growing, healthy ecumenism. Ecumenism focuses on commonalities rather than on differences. Like denominationalism, ecumenism has the advantage of connecting churches to the wider movement of God, drawing on shared liturgies and traditions, centering on a common mission and purpose, and developing financial resources and leadership. We have a rich history of great saints who have turned the world upside down. We are standing on their shoulders.

To paraphrase Paul: these things happened to serve as an example, and they were written to teach us, on whom the ends of the ages have come (1 Corinthians 10:14). The power and presence of the coming Kingdom are already here, operative in the church. Although we await the full revelation in God's final and decisive act, He has given us the Scriptures (both Old and New Testaments) to provide us examples and models. Paul is just one of those examples, but what an excellent example he is! If we were to take his gospel and his strategies, and if we were to walk boldly in the Spirit as did he, then future generations might say about us: "They turned the world upside down."

Section Three // **The Evolving Church of Today**

From the 1ˢᵀ into the 21ˢᵀ Century

by Robert Creech

Emerging Is Difficult

Emerging is difficult. The butterfly endures metamorphosis and exhausts itself in the process. The cries of the human infant emerging from the womb are simultaneous deep breaths of life and not-so-silent protests against the change he or she has had to accomplish. The child's cries are preceded by the agony of the mother as well. When fresh forms have emerged among the people of God over the centuries, the outcries of the previous generation at the birth pangs has always blended with the exhilarating cries of the present one.

Exiles from Babylon returned to the rubble of Jerusalem to rebuild their homes, reestablish their city, reconstruct their temple, restore their religion, and renew their lives. The birth pangs of the first step into the future were felt as the foundation of the temple was completed. Ezra reports the result of their labor:

> The people were making all kinds of noise and joyful sounds about the goodness of the Lord. They were full of praise when they saw that the foundation was laid for the new temple. They were remembering the former days in the previous temple in all its glory. The joyous sounds were mixed with weeping, and people heard the sounds miles away. The old wineskins of preexilic Judaism were no longer, and the new wine of revival was beginning to ferment.

Old Forms Die

This pattern of old forms dying and new forms rising is a theme throughout the story of God's people. After the exodus, the people of God lamented leaving their lives in Egypt (Numbers 11:4-5), as if they had never seen a day of slavery there. Dynasties rose and fell. Empires flowed in and out like the tides. Ultimately, history shook with the birth pangs of a new kind of kingdom, the kingdom of God. Israel's institutions and traditions quaked in the presence of Jesus, and they successfully conspired to take His life. The Jews were, in Jesus' words, addicted to tradition. They loved the old, aged wine better (Luke 5:39).

New Forms Rise

Jesus warned the Jews that something new was coming that was far more powerful than the old. It would start small like a mustard seed or like yeast in a batch of dough, but it would spread powerfully. It would be new wine, but it would be the choicest ever uncorked, and the old wineskins could never hold it.

By the time labor was complete, the temple and the holy city would be demolished. Israel's institutional religion would yield to the fulfillment of the prophets who saw the nations (Gentiles) streaming to Jerusalem. God would make all things new (Revelation 21:5).

The first seven chapters of Acts are the birth narratives of the church in Jerusalem. When the church first emerged, it did so from the womb of Judaism. Its birth was painful for the mother and challenging for the child. The newborn church cried out the good news of the resurrection of the Messiah in the holy city where He had been nailed to a cross. It learned to walk and talk in the temple courts and courtrooms of its mother. The remainder of Acts is about this new church spreading throughout the Roman Empire.[1]

Jewish Roots

Judaism not only gave birth to the church, but she also passed on her heritage. In its infancy, the church was thoroughly Jewish. It worshiped at the temple. It observed the designated hours of prayer. It attended the synagogue and kept kosher. The church did not see itself as a new religion—Christianity. It saw itself as a group of faithful, observant Jews who had found the Messiah in Jesus and was experiencing the joys of the age to come—forgiveness, the Spirit, community, and power. For a time.

Children eventually leave home. At least, that's the plan. They emerge from the womb into the parents' arms and then emerge from their arms into the world. The church did not leave home willingly. It was too comfortable. Like the Hebrews in Egypt, it became necessary for God to "stir the nest" and push them out (Deuteronomy 32:11). Persecution drove portions of the church from the city of its birth, pushing them into contact with the Gentile world for the first time.

---

1 Here the modern institutional church is spoken of as "parent" or "mother," and of the postmodern emerging church as "child." The intent is not to patronize or to imply some kind of immaturity on the part of the young churches. They have "emerged" from the institutional, evangelical church (the parent church). The parent-child metaphor represents the natural and beautiful cycle of life by which one generation (of people or of the church) emerges from another, connected powerfully by a loving dependence at first, then moving out in a connected independence.

Encountering the Gentiles

Some of these who left home were bold enough to tell the good news they had learned to the Gentiles they encountered. They discovered that when these uncircumcised Gentiles placed their trust in Jesus the Messiah, God poured out His Spirit on them, just as He had done for Jewish believers on the church's birthday. Before they could be circumcised, before they could be baptized, God accepted these Gentiles and adopted them into the family as if they had been born into it.

This was the issue that led to the full emergence of the early church. This was the issue that raised the questions of salvation and ethics, interpretation of Scripture and holy history, ecclesiology and missiology. On what basis does God accept Gentiles? What is it that they must *believe* in order to be part of His family? What is it they must *do*? What is the essential message, the *kerygma* that we must proclaim? What is the place of our traditional practices such as circumcision, baptism, and diet? What about participation with idols, such as eating the meat offered to them in their temples? What about the legendary immorality of the Gentile world? What do we require? What do we advise? What is the essential gospel? What is the essential church?

Becoming a Fellowship of Community

The church faced this final emergence from Judaism into the Hellenistic world with few resources in their possession. But they were valuable ones. They had the Hebrew Scriptures of their faith, full of stories and songs and oracles. They had the presence of the Spirit to guide their honest quest for truth. They had the loving trust in one another, called *koinonia* or "fellowship," that had marked their experience as community. They had the testimony of missionaries like Peter, Paul, and Barnabas, who had been among the Gentiles for years and could verify what God was doing there.

Packing these few God-given possessions, the church made the decision that the kingdom of God required them to leave the familiarity and sanctuary of their traditions in Judaism. They would take their faith, much of their understanding of whom God is, their Scriptures, and the promised Spirit of the New Covenant, and they would launch out despite the jealous protest of the one in whose home they had been born and nurtured.

Jesus had seen this break on the horizon. The day would come, He had told them, when they would have to choose Him over father and mother. The day would come when synagogues would be places they received floggings rather than instruction. The day would come when the temple would be dismantled. The day would come when they would be making disciples of all the nations (mainly, the Gentiles).

It was in this context that the first church truly emerged. When they did, they entered new territory. They had so much to figure out. The New Testament epistles are mostly accounts of this struggle. Making disciples of the Messiah out of formerly idol-worshiping Gentiles was more than a challenge.

Growing Pains for the Young Church

The growing pains of the first church is the story that the young church and the institutional church of the 21st century need to attend to, for it is being relived in the midst of us. We would be foolish either as mother or child not to pay attention to the account we have been blessed to receive.

Just as our first-century sisters and brothers had to move from the safety, security, and familiarity of Judaism in order to be true to their mission and calling to follow Jesus, some 21st century believers have experienced the restlessness that accompanies a call. A call that is much like Abram's call to leave his home and go to a new land which God would show him.

This time the call is not to a foreign *place*, but to a foreign *time*. The home was the institutional church of the modern, Western world. The 20th-century version was marked by professional ordained clergy prepared in seminaries that were sometimes denominational training facilities. Programs and buildings were necessities, part of the very identity of church. In this world, "church" is not who you are, it is where you go. The paradigm is centuries old in the West and difficult to leave. Missions belonged to the select few, the missionaries who were willing to uproot and travel to some distant place. Even in traditions that espoused "the priesthood of all believers," professional clergy were viewed as a class of Christian different from "the laity." All these things and more were part of the "essential church" of the modern, Western world.

A New Christian Ethic

But what if the ancient gospel was taken to a world that differs radically from the perspectives and assumptions of modernity? What if some decide to pack their bags and leave home, bound for the mission field of a postmodern world? What do they take with them? What do they leave behind? Which of those practices that were part of the nurturing of well-meaning parents do they no longer retain? What language and expressions of their faith do they determine are cultural husk rather than gospel kernel? What do Christian ethics look like in this new world? How does worship take form? What does it take to have essential church?

Intentional

Essential church is *intentional*. The story in Acts is about people who choose to be part of a movement, as Barnabas and Saul chose to sail to Cyprus. A church is not an accidental gathering of people. In a locality, believers in Jesus choose to associate their lives with each other around Him. They know what they are doing. They *intend* to be a church.

Spirit Filled

Essential church is *filled with the Spirit*. The church of Acts could not have survived without the Spirit of God. Some have even suggested the book should be called "The Acts of the Holy Spirit" rather than "The Acts of the Apostles." Church is a work of the Holy Spirit in the lives of God's people. It is not a mere social movement. In the premodern world, the modern world, or the postmodern world, the church learns to depend on the real and powerful presence of the Spirit of God making Jesus Christ real among them. No Spirit, no church.

Community

Essential church is a *community*. People belong to God and to each other. Luke's word to describe this community in Acts is *koinonia*. Dietrich Bonhoeffer called it "life together." The sharing of life, goods, trials, and hope is essential to the meaning of church. Authentic community transcends social and cultural barriers. It crosses generations. It reconciles enemies. Essential church takes seriously the corporate dimension of life.

Following Jesus

Essential church is about *following Jesus Christ*. It understands Christianity as a life to be lived, not merely as a set of doctrines to be believed. The practices of Jesus and the teachings of Jesus are cherished and applied. The church of Acts was all about following Jesus, going where He goes, doing what He does. Their earliest identity was as "followers of the Way" (Acts 9:2). Jesus' commission to make disciples also included the call to teach the "practices and postures that I have taught you, and show them how to follow the commands I have laid down for you" (Matthew 28:20). Part of following Jesus involves learning and living from the Scriptures Jesus read and quoted (the Old Testament) and from those that describe Him and His people (the New Testament).

Engaging the Mission

Essential church is about *engaging the mission of God.* Church is ultimately not about us. It is about God and what God is engaging in the world. We align our lives with His mission when we decide to follow Jesus and sign on with His people, the church. Without the mission of God, the church would not have been born. Without the mission of God, the church loses its reason for being.

As a generation moves into the future, these are the essential elements they take with them. Everything else is optional. Forms, traditions, ways of talking about our faith, structures, and organization are among *adiaphora*, the indifferent things. These things must be worked out through an ongoing conversation between the gospel and the culture.

The experience of a child's transitions into the world is painful and difficult for the parent as well. When the child leaves home, parents often hope they will take with them *everything* they have been taught. Watching them become individuals, who make their own decisions and choose their own ways, is not easy for the parent.

Three Options

The institutional church experiences the pain of emergence differently. But this church has choices about how it responds. Too often the response is reactionary, not unlike a parent with a child. This new thing must be stopped. It is not what we have known. If it is different, it threatens us. The reactions are reflexes, instinctual responses erupting from below the level of consciousness. After the reaction, we develop our "reasons," lest we appear irrational. Just as Mother Judaism had a difficult time seeing in her child the fulfillment of her dreams, so the institutional church sometimes has a difficult time recognizing the mission of God in young churches struggling to connect culturally with their own generation.

The parental church can *choose to criticize* and attempt to squelch the movement among her children. Judaism tried that. Like most parent-children conflicts, the opposition of the parent only entrenched the children in their commitment to the way they had chosen! It would be possible for the parental church to cut off from the emerging movement, to throw up its hands and *choose to ignore* it, going on with its familiar ways, hoping that someday the child will come back home. While that would be an improvement over conflict, it still does not represent the most attractive option.

A third possibility is open. The parental church can *choose to bless* its children and stay involved appropriately in their lives. Rather than chiding them, criticizing them, or giving up on them, parents can learn to know their grown children as adults. Parents do not have to adopt their children's ways, or even like their ways. But they can seek to understand them and bless them and help them. This is a relationship the parental, institutional, evangelical church can choose to have with the emerging church. It can be instrumental in helping safeguard the children's well-being.

Letting Our Children Go

The Lebanese poet, Kahlil Gibran, wrote this about letting go of children:

> Your children are not your children.
> They are the sons and daughters of Life's longing for itself.
> They come through you but not from you,
> And though they are with you, yet they belong not to you.
> You may give them your love but not your thoughts.
> For they have their own thoughts.
> You may house their bodies but not their souls,
> For their souls dwell in the house of tomorrow, which you
> cannot visit, not even in your dreams.
> You may strive to be like them, but seek not to make them like
> you.
> For life goes not backward nor tarries with yesterday.
> You are the bows from which your children as living arrows are
> sent forth.
> The archer sees the mark upon the path of the infinite, and He
> bends you with His might that His arrows may go swift and far.

Let your bending in the archer's hand be for gladness;
For even as He loves the arrow that flies, so He loves also the bow that is stable.[2]

Challenge, Correct

Just as ancient Judaism could have seen the followers of the Way as people who could reach Gentiles in ways their traditional forms never could, so the institutional church can bless the efforts of the emerging church to reach a world that parental churches never will.

Leaders of the parental church need to stay connected with leaders of the emerging church. Conversation, dialogue, mutual prayer, and encouragement would be the most profound expressions of the power of the Kingdom that is among us. There is a genuine humility in these young churches that often asks to be challenged, even corrected, lest this experiment in Christian ministry and mission wander from the path. That same humility would be appropriate on the part of the parental church, learning to see its mission through the eyes of another generation.

Chapter Twenty-Nine

Acts is well known as an unfinished story. At the end of the book, Paul is imprisoned in Rome, proclaiming the kingdom of God and teaching about the ultimate authority, Jesus, the promised Liberating King, "with great confidence and with no hindrance" (Acts 28:31). In the Greek text, the story ends, oddly, with an adverb, "unhinderly." We do not learn the outcome of Paul's trial. We have questions that remain unanswered. We do not hear a nice, rounding off of the account with "and they lived happily ever after."

Perhaps the reason for this unusual ending is that the story is not over. Acts 28 closes a chapter but does not end the story. Chapter 29 continues with the church through the ages. Our chapter is still being written. How will it end? Will the new birth of an emergent movement take the gospel of Jesus, the Liberating King, powerfully into a postmodern world with great confidence and with no hindrance? Will the questions of essential church and essential gospel be answered adequately to bear the life and power of Jesus into the future without losing a generation? We will see.

---

2 Kahlil Gibran, *The Prophet* (New York: Alfred A. Knopf, 1968), p. 17.

Catching the Big One

by Evan Lauer

Surfing and the Early Church

All history is not worth repeating, but there is so much we can learn from our past. Unless you are caught up in church growth, church culture, and many of the trappings today's church life offers, it's hard *not* to look back fondly to the Book of Acts, particularly as the church first began in the first chapters of Acts.

The early church was underground, not yet famous, and always searching for those "followers of the Way." They met often to share what little they had and to encourage each other in this new religion. They may have been a minority in the ancient world, but they knew they had encountered the truth in Jesus and were going to figure out a way to share that truth no matter the cost.

The founders of the early church are similar to those who birthed the sport of surfing in California. Surfers literally traveled up and down the coast looking for fellow surfers and were excited to meet them. Surfing then was an underground, renegade sport. Only the hard-core-committed surfed. They met in small groups, shared what they had, and spurred each other on in this new sport. They believed in the surfing lifestyle so much they were willing to be relegated to the fringes of society to pursue their passion.

The same thing happened to the early believers; they were persecuted for their beliefs. Yet what drove them to overcome the odds was their knowledge of the truth. Many in the community had seen Jesus with their own eyes, heard Him teach, and watched Him heal the sick. Because of their experiences, we believe there was an authenticity to this early form of Christian faith that most churches have lost today. We can't help but consider the year A.D. 313 as a dark spot in church history. That is the year the persecution began to lift and the dependence upon God for survival was not as great. With the Edict of Milan, Christianity became a legitimate religion. Constantine stopped the persecution of Christians. Anyone could live a rather safe "Christian" life if they remained within Constantine's empire. The "church" emerged from the underground, left house-to-house meetings, and embraced the use of larger buildings called "basilicas." In some cases, this may have been necessary due to growth. But these may well have been some of the first steps that led people to view the "church" as a building instead of as a people.

Later, in A.D. 392, Christianity became the sole religion of the empire. At first, this might seem like good news, these early steps to legitimacy and freedom. But the fact is this: the Christian church is at her best when she is not the established religion. Although it seems counterintuitive, the church has often thrived under persecution. She has flourished when she has confronted culture rather than embraced or accommodated it. There's an old proverb: In times of prosperity, no altars smoke. That is not a bad summary of church history. When the church has wielded power, or when she has seemed to fit in well with the rest of society, the vitality that comes from depending on God is absent. On the other hand, when the church has been persecuted by the powers or when she has stood against culture, her life has been full and authentic. This doesn't mean, of course, that we should seek persecution or develop a martyr's complex. What it does mean is that we should be wary of trying to accommodate society rather than engaging and redeeming it. Our mission is not to overlay western culture with a thin veneer of Christian values; our mission is to rescue people out of western culture, realizing it is a lost cause. The Scripture is clear: the "world" is passing away, and only that part of the world that has been rescued out of darkness will last.

Without romanticizing the past too much, we can see common principles in both the early church and the early days of surfing that we can apply to how we worship—and ride the waves—today. Maybe where the church is today—that is, the Western ideal of church growth and its fascination with facilities and programs—is not what God originally intended. Going back to the cornerstone of the church's beginning, "back when it was pure," will tell us how a living church should act.

Being Totally Immersed

For most surfers, there is an aspect of total immersion with the surfing lifestyle. Many surfers sacrifice certain amenities to be near the ocean and the sport they love so much. The early Christians had no choice but to do the same thing. Following Peter's sermon, the people's response was immediate and all encompassing. These early Christians were "cut to the heart." For them to repent, be baptized, receive the Holy Spirit, devote themselves to the apostles' teaching, fellowship, break bread, and pray meant total immersion in this new way of life.

You may wonder how they "did church." They stuck to the basics: love and service. They held everything in common—sold their possessions for the common good and gave to anyone who had needs. They worked together as a community of believers to spread the message of Jesus. Their days were saturated with fellowship. Worshiping was time spent together celebrating their new faith in the simplest way. They would meet in the temple courts every day, break bread in their homes, and eat together with glad and sincere hearts, praising God and enjoying each others' company. If that could be said of our churches today, then the world would notice. After all, who wouldn't want to be involved with a group like this?

One of the great aspects of surfing is becoming totally immersed in the ocean. It's like getting baptized every time. Time in the water is called "sessions," kind of like going to therapy sessions. Most surfers are so immersed in the sport and lifestyle that it becomes their religion. Many surfers say they don't need to go to church. They fondly look out at the great sea and say, "This is my church right here." And certainly they are closer than some to knowing the true church. Whether they realize it or not, paddling out into the ocean, entering something so much bigger than themselves with nothing but trust, love, and a board, *is* a spiritual experience that takes a lot of faith. What they are saying is, "I may not be able to comprehend fully the entire ocean, but I can still get in it and experience it." It's the same way in our relationship with God. He is big and mysterious, but through Jesus, we can enter into a relationship with Him that leads us to our own experience of God. But it's about so much more than just a personal experience with God. God created us for relationships and community.

Surfing alone is not just lonely, but it also greatly increases the odds of becoming shark bait. It's great when there is a nice, small pack of guys in the water. All can share waves, tell stories, and enjoy God's creation. It's the same with church life; we were not created to "surf alone." We read in Acts 2:47, "Day after day the Lord added to their number everyone who was experiencing liberation." There is no doubt that God intended for us to live in a community. In Acts, many believed and thousands were added to their number "that day alone . . . 3,000" (Acts 2:41), but was such growth the norm? Not likely. That is the essence of church life—simplicity—letting the Lord do His work and adding daily to our numbers.

The Bible is our guide for living, so the pattern for church life today has to be based on the early church in Acts. How the church gets there is going to take all of us roaming the coast, grabbing our boards, and taking a faith-filled jump into the water together. We must be willing to band together through the biggest waves. Know that, in the end, God is so much bigger and greater than we can understand or even fathom—He has always had a plan. And there is no other way for the church to live than to be immersed in Him.

Too Busy to Become

Why did we let life get to the point where everyone is "so-o busy"? And how did things get to the point where pastors are so wrapped up in church administration/church life/church staff stuff that they can barely allow time for a two-hour lunch with someone from their church? Or what about investing quality time in the community and being known for serving the needs of others instead of always assuming everyone will come to the great show we present during our grand worship services? It's hard to picture the early church's apostles being "so-o busy" that they couldn't spend time with their people. The very nature of true fellowship, breaking bread, and prayer allows time for living life together.

In most churches, everyone hangs out after the service—catching up on life, eating yummy snacks, and watching all the kids run around. When they start to take the extra time to fellowship for a while after church, you know they are making this church their home; they want to invest in the lives of others. This is when true community in the body of Christ starts to happen for a new person in a church. People need to become a part of the faith community for reasons greater than the "great worship service"; they need to see the Lord adding to the body daily as in the first church.

Obviously, God deserves our praise, a corporate time of worship, prayer, teaching, communion, and reflection. But people are necessary in the church—for it would be impossible without them—to fellowship, to talk about life, and to share concerns and prayer requests. We often place too much emphasis on planning the "ultimate worship service" when we should be focusing more on the quality of the time we spend in each other's presence. Unfortunately, most people today expect a greatly preplanned worship service, or they don't consider it "real church." The early church gatherings must have been utterly simplistic. Sunday morning gatherings should be more focused on getting together, sharing a meal, discussing our faith, and serving the poor.

A New Way of Missions

by Andrew Jones

Constant Questioning

Here's the scene: You and I are hanging out in a strange city, eating strange food that we swore we'd never eat. It is hot outside, but we are sheltered from the sun, engrossed in dialogue about the expansion of the church and who is leading it. The atmosphere is mixed. On one hand, there is a sense of despondency. Previous expectations were not met, and there has been more hardship than we ever anticipated. Our missionaries are coming home. We feel spent. We are constantly questioning: "Did we do something wrong?"

But there is hope. There are stories and dreams. Large numbers. Fast movements. Things we would not have believed, even if we were told. The ecclesial center under our benevolent watch has shifted out to the margins. The places where we sent missionaries are sending them back. Unknown leaders have risen up to lead them. To lead us. One of them is from Africa. Everything is changing so fast. The new believers do not revere our heroes. They do not own our taboos. But there is a spiritual vibrancy here that eludes us back home. We knew it once, a long time ago. The blessing of God is noticeably with them and, it seems, is diminishing among some of us.

Are we outmoded? Do we need to be upgraded? Is God wiping us off?

Is God Starting Anew?

I am speaking, here, at a global missions gathering in Johannesburg, South Africa. Leaders from all over the world have come to pray and discuss the mission of God, which is now squarely in the hands of the two/thirds world. The gathering in South Africa begins, and I am reminded of how different things are today from two decades ago, when I first left my home to be a missionary.

Dr. Stephen Steele, Vice President for Global Research and Strategy for a large foundation, gives the opening address entitled "Is God Doing Something New?"[3] His answer is "Yes." The global church scene is radically different and is

---

3 Dr. Stephen Steele, "Is God Doing Something New?" address to Global Associates Conference (Johannesburg, South Africa, 2006).

continually transforming. New things that are impacting it include the exponential growth of the church, the challenge of complexity, impact of globalization and communications, persecution, the shaking up of world religions, the power of information and technology (Internet), an emphasis on holistic missions, and the changing reality of the two/thirds world church and indigenous leaders.

The Shift

In some ways, I am part of the shift. If Dr. Steele is correct in saying that globalization and communications are key to this transition we find ourselves in, then I am part of this shift from the old to the new. My kids were born on three continents. They are part of this shift with me. We are participators in the internet culture, connected globally, able to express ourselves in the self-publishing revolution through new media.

The Indian lady sitting behind me is part of that shift. She and her husband have started 14,000 churches in the last decade. Their churches do not have buildings nor Sunday services. Their model is more similar to the early church in the Book of Acts.

Ngwiza Mnkandla sits near the front. He is part of that shift. Born in Zimbabwe, he now heads up DAWN Ministries International. A few years ago, we were discussing the postmodern shift in African missions. Ngwiza informed me that the missionaries who first came to Zimbabwe were unable to deal with the supernatural and the demonic powers. This is another gift that the African church offers the global church.

My Brazilian friend, Olgavaro Bastos, is part of that shift. He is representing the vibrant emerging churches all over South America. They are connected to us, but not dependent. In many ways they seem healthier than our churches in the USA. After telling him how much I respected his ministry, I told him clearly that the South American emerging churches were in no way inferior to those of the North, and that we need to learn from them. When I prayed for him, he wept on my shoulder.

Power Shift

"Previously, the evangelical movement possibly influenced by the rational bent of the modern era, focused so much on the content of the gospel in terms of the atoning work of Christ that it may have ignored this aspect of the power of the gospel. This was clearly an inadequate presentation of the gospel" (Ajith Fernando).[4]

Power flows differently here. Hierarchies are modular and dynamic. Emergent organizational forces are at work. Knowledge is stored, retrieved, and called up at will. Social communities are forming online. Church is simple and complex at the same time. And the temptation remains to run ahead with the new without being held back by the old. But the way of Jesus involves change and continuity, shifting to keep up with the Spirit while holding to what is timeless. Blessing the new and honoring the old.

God Prepares the Way

Apostles are bearers of gifts, not salesmen of products. God gives the gift purchased by Christ, and the Spirit prepares the reception. Jesus is both the message and model of mission (Ajith Fernando).[5] Where the gift is refused, the givers move on until they find a more receptive environment.

In my ministry journeys of helping establish new works in various cities, I can't say that I have physically shaken the dust off my feet, or made a prophetic announcement to those who refused God's ministry through me. But there was one time when it worked out that way.

In the late 1990s, I was asked by Chris Seay to come to Austin, Texas, to explore the possibility of ministry among the street kids and "postmoderns," as they were called back then. Our work in San Francisco was based around this mobile demographic, and Austin was part of the national circuit. After spending time on the streets, I determined to bring the challenge to the traditional churches first and perhaps find a historical link to bridge the old with the new. I decided the biggest Baptist church in the area would be worth approaching.

But a few days before visiting their Sunday service, an unfortunate miscommunication had sullied my reputation among their leadership who assumed I was requesting funding from one of their members. This seemed to be a huge setback, but I figured that God had allowed the miscommunication to happen for a reason. That Sunday, I attended a different church, Austin First Baptist, a 150-year-

---

4 Ajith Fernando, "God: The Source, The Originator, and the End of Mission," *Global Missiology for the 21st Century: The Iguassu Dialogue*, ed. William D. Taylor (Grand Rapids, MI: Baker Academic, 2000).

5 Ajith Fernando, "God: The Source, The Originator, and the End of Mission," *Global Missiology for the 21st Century: The Iguassu Dialogue*, ed. William D. Taylor (Grand Rapids, MI: Baker Academic, 2000).

old congregation in the heart of the city. I had no idea how to approach the senior pastor. But at the end of the sermon, surprisingly, he walked straight up to me and asked, "Are you the guy I just read about in the newspaper? A deacon's mother in Dallas sent me the article and this week I was wondering how I might contact you. Could you come to speak to my leaders and deacons next Tuesday? You see, God has placed us in the heart of this city and we want to figure out how to minister to the young people here. Maybe you can help us?"

That Spirit-guided redirection led to an exciting adventure in partnership resulting in the establishment of new ministries and a number of international roundtable events.

I'm not saying there were no tension points along the way—there were issues. Candle wax was spilled on carpets. At a worship event called Ecclesia, the DJ's fog machines set off the smoke alarms, and the fire brigade was running through the dance floor with helmets and hoses. Despite the mayhem, the event continued unabated. But grace abounded, lives were changed, and bridges were maintained between old and young.

Here's what Pastor Doug Keenan remembers about the intergenerational aspect:

> I will never forget the image of a 90-year-old Doctor of Theology and former President of the North American Baptist Convention sitting on the floor in the midst of our large atrium surrounded by a half dozen young people with glittered hair, tattoos, and multiple body piercings banging on bongos as a part of a spontaneous drum circle. If postmodern ministry could bring together those extremes, then I realized we needed to find ways to increase our involvement with this form of ministry.[6]

Missional

I have come to see that mission comes from God and our role is to participate with Him in what He is doing. Mission is "shaped by God's heart" (Milfred Minatrea)[7] and flows from Him to us. We should expect that the missionary God

---

6 Douglas R. Keenan, "Leading First Baptist Church, Austin, Texas to Discover New Ways to Share the Gospel in a Postmodern Environment." Partial fulfillment of requirements for the Doctor of Ministry (Waco, Texas: Baylor University, 2005).

7 Milfred Minatrea, *Shaped by God's Heart: The Passion and Practices of Missional Churches* (San Francisco, CA: Wiley, an imprint of Jossey Bass, 2004).

who initiates ministry would send us to the right place at the right time. Jesus sends us to a ripe harvest where there will be people of peace prepared by the Spirit to receive our gift and offer their own. This plays out on a civic level as well as domestic. There will be geographical areas and institutions favorable to us while others will be hardened against us. This forces us into a strategy of waiting on God, fervent prayer, research, and risk taking in personal relationships.

Samuel Escobar put it this way: "Traditional mission models inherited from the Christendom mentality and the colonial era are now obsolete. It is time for a paradigm shift that will come from a salutary return to the Word of God... The future demands more models of non-paternalistic holistic missions. An incarnational approach modeled by Jesus and Paul is the key."[8] There are some who might argue with Escobar on this, but they would all be white, Anglo, middle-class men who live in wealthy countries that used to control the global mission enterprise.

A New Generation of Leaders

How do you validate the new leaders without isolating the former power-holders? How do you bridge the new things into their historical roots without adding unnecessary baggage to those on the front line?

My struggle is Peter's struggle. He has become convinced, through the vision God gave him and the evidence of the Spirit among the Gentile believers, that God is doing something new. He needs to report it to the Jewish elders in a way that maintains unity but communicates the importance of the shift so that everyone gets on board.

My struggle is Luke's struggle. Luke is recording the account of this shift. He is concerned with continuity in the midst of change. Unlike Matthew, who accentuates the hypocrisy of the Pharisees and implicates the Jews in Jesus' death, Luke steers away from potential rifts with the Jews toward an unbroken outworking of God through His people—the Jews first and then the Gentiles also. Luke's account gives validation to the new wave of Gentile mission leaders and reminds them of their roots in Jewish stock. They will not be "Israel 2.0." They will not form a "new Israel," argues David Bosch,[9] but rather a "true Israel," a part of the new aggregation of God.

---

8 Samuel Escobar, "The Global Scenario at the Turn of the Century," *Global Missiology for the 21st Century: The Iguassu Dialogue,* ed. William D. Taylor (Grand Rapids, MI: Baker Academic, 2000).

9 David Jacobus Bosch, *Transforming Mission: Paradigm Shift in Theology of Mission* (Maryknoll, New York: Oris Books, 1991).

Participation by all in the mission of God.

Harmony—Peace—Integrity—Posterity—Honor
Givenness—Cost—Risk—Advancement

Fellowship of The Woodlands

A Case Study by Kerry Shook

The True Ministry of Christ

I love what I do. I pastor an amazing congregation, but some days I wrestle with deep questions about what it means to live out the true ministry of Christ described in the Book of Acts. Our church is committed to all kinds of ministries on our campus, throughout the city, and across the globe, but we devote a great deal of time, energy, and resources to our youth ministry. The Woodlands is the closest thing to a suburban utopia outside the city of Houston as you can get. It looks like a place of beauty, safety, and prosperity; but for teenagers, it is a dangerous place. These kids are struggling to find their true identities, and many are getting lost in the dangers of academic competition, substance abuse, and sexual promiscuity. All of this has led to an alarming number of students who are clinically depressed and a frightening rate of suicide.

I was discussing these struggles recently with one of my teenage sons when he questioned my heart for youth ministry. "You don't really care about my friends," he said. "If you did, you would spend more time with us talking about these things." He made a valid point. He longed to see me enter this battle with him and devote my own time and energy to the struggles of the young men and women in our community. So now I am leading a weekly small group with my sons to provide a place for safe conversation with their friends. The ministries of our church were great, but I realized that they deserved more. As I lead Fellowship of The Woodlands, I am constantly finding these places that call for more of my heart, commitment, and devotion to the gospel being lived out among those who seem to have everything but who need more than what they have.

The rapid growth of the early church reminds me of some common myths in today's church that must be dispelled. There are two major myths about fast-growing churches.

Myth Number One

There's no way they can grow that fast, legitimately. They are either watering down the gospel, or not calling people to true discipleship. The early church shows us that nothing could be further from the truth. The disciples preached the gospel of Jesus Christ and called people to repentance, and the church grew exponentially.

Myth Number Two

Fast-growing churches have got it all together—they must be perfect. Many pastors in small churches look at the pastor of a fast-growing church and think, *He must always know just the right thing to do,* or, *His church must never have any of the problems we have.* The early church shows us again that nothing could be further from the truth. Look in Acts 6. The first church had a big problem: some of the widows were being left out of the food distribution. The point is that fast-growing churches face struggles, problems, and challenges just like many other churches do. As our church has grown, we have made repeated mistakes, allowed people to fall through the cracks, and dropped the ball far too often.

A Living Example

I am a living example that pastors of fast-growing churches are vulnerable to the pitfalls of human nature. Twelve years ago, my wife and I started Fellowship of The Woodlands. We gathered with 15 people, and I shared with them how exciting this church would be. They got so excited only eight of them came back the next week. I had lost half the congregation in one week. I did the math, and even though I'm not very good at math, I realized that if this trend continued, our church would be done in just one more week. My wife and I were so discouraged, but it was at that time we just gave the church completely to God. We said, "Lord, if Your goal is that one person comes to You and their eternal destiny is changed, then it will all be worth it." All I've done for the past 12 years is preach God's Word in a practical and relevant way week in and week out, and somehow God changes lives. The reason our church has grown to 13,000 attendees is that Jesus Christ changes lives and God determines all growth. A pastor's call is to be faithful, not to produce the results. The size of a church is no big deal because it's all up to God.

Sometimes when pastors or church leaders see the problems that growth causes, they try to put the brakes on the Holy Spirit's momentum. I remember when our church had about 200 attendees. A leader in our church came to me and said, "I think we should stop growing and just focus on growing these people strong in Christ." I said, "You're right that we should grow these people strong in Christ, but we should also keep reaching out." Then I asked him, "How would you like me to stop the church from growing? Lock the doors and tell people to go away? We've always said God will determine our growth, and we'll keep the doors open."

Example of the Early Church

The early church had to make structural changes to meet the needs of the growing membership. We are constantly making changes in our structure to meet the changing needs in our church. Many times, like the church of Acts, we don't see the needed changes until we have a problem staring us in the face. God always uses the problem to bring about productive change. The disciples knew they each would make the greatest impact in their areas of giftedness, which was leading and feeding the Word to the church. My goal is to spend 80 percent of my time using 20 percent of my gifts, which for me is leading and feeding. The disciples picked seven leaders to organize and administrate the ministry issues that arose. Our goal is to constantly pursue, pick, and promote leaders to minister by using their gifts. The people are the ministers, and it's our job to train them and encourage them. It's our goal as pastors to not bottleneck the church from growing by trying to do it all ourselves.

Our fast-growing church certainly has problems associated with growth, but I believe the impact we make in our community and world far outweigh any problems that spring up. We always say, "A big church can make a big difference" if we come together to make an impact. Every fall we impact the community with what we call a "Campaign for Kindness." For six weeks the whole church is mobilized to minister to the community. We rake leaves, sweep driveways, wash cars, and clean garages for just about everyone in the community, with nothing expected in return. We also repair houses and fill food banks for the under-resourced. When everyone in our church touches the lives of 10 people with the love of Christ, we touch over 100,000 people in just six weeks. A big church can make a big difference.

A couple of years ago, I kicked off our campaign of kindness with a message on ministering to the poor. At the end of the service, I told our members that the greatest need in the homeless shelters were shoes and underwear because they mostly receive blankets. I challenged our people to leave their shoes on the stage before they left and to walk outside in socks or bare feet to feel what some people feel every day, if they were led to do so. Our people left over 4,500 pairs of shoes on that stage. It solved the shoe problem in Houston for a few months, but it did more for us than anyone else. The next year we gave 13,000 pair of underwear (new and still in the package!).

Continuing Struggle

I will continue to struggle with the challenges of discipling a large congregation; but I am more convinced than ever that a big church can make a big difference. The truth is we are all a working part of one church, and we share this journey with Paul, Peter, Augustine, Patrick, Luther, Wesley, Spurgeon, and Bono.

Section Four // **exerpt from *The Last Eyewitness***

Chapter 2

Learning to Serve

*M*y name is John. My father's name was Zebedee. We made our living by fishing on the Sea of Galilee. I am the last eyewitness to the life of Jesus. All the rest are gone, some long gone. Many died years ago, tragically young, the victims of Roman cruelty and persecution. For some reason Jesus chose me to live to be an old man. In fact, some in my community have taken to calling me "the elder." I suppose that's because there are others with the name "John" in our community.

I am the inspiration behind the Fourth Gospel. These are my stories, recorded, told to you by my disciples. I'm proud of what they have done. Me? I've never done much writing. But the story is truly mine.

You see my hands. They've been hurting for the past 20 years now. I couldn't hold a pen even if I wanted to. Not that I was ever good at writing. I was a fisherman so my hands were calloused. I could tie ropes, mend nets, and pull the oars, but never make a decent *xi* (Greek letter). So we used secretaries when we wanted to write. There was always a bright young man around it seems, ready to take a letter or help us put pen to papyrus. Even our brother Paul used secretaries—Tertius, Luke, and Titus—just to name a few.

John the Evangelist

My eyes are too weak to read anymore. I can't remember the last time I could see well enough to read a letter or even see the inscriptions. So one of the brothers (I call them, "my little children") reads to me. They are all very gracious to me in my old age, compiling my stories, bringing me food, laughing at my jokes, and caring for my most intimate needs. Time is taking its toll on me though. I rarely have the energy to tell the old stories and preach entire sermons. Instead, I simply remind them of Christ's most vital command, saying as loudly as I can, "Little children, love one another." I repeat this phrase quite often.

Jesus had this group of guys. He called us "the twelve." We traveled with Him, spent time with Him, ate with Him, and listened to Him talk about God's kingdom. We watched Him perform miracles. These weren't the tricks like you see in the market or attempts at magic you hear about at shrines. These were what I call signs. Something was breaking into our darkness. These signs pointed to a greater reality most people didn't even know was there. In the other Gospels they call them miracles or works of power. We've decided to tell you about select signs because these, more than any, revealed the true glory of this Man.

Jesus wanted us to be His family, a different kind of community. We figured it out later. By calling us "the twelve," Jesus was creating a new people of God. God was doing something new, like the prophets had promised. We were living at the center of history. From now on everything would be different. This made us feel special, proud, and sometimes arrogant. We'd sometimes jockey for Jesus' attention. Even within "the twelve" some were closer to Jesus. He had this "inner circle" of sorts. I was part of it. Peter, Andrew, James, and I were with Jesus at times when the other fellows had to stay behind. I'm not sure why He picked me. Because of that, I knew He loved me and I would have a special place with Him.

Jesus also had other students. Not all of them stayed. Some came and some went. I don't really know how many people in all. One time He sent out seventy of us to proclaim the good news and heal in His name. He even let women be His students. Most people don't know this, but women were among those who helped support us financially (Lk 8). At a time when people said it was a shame for a man to be supported by women, Jesus took their help and took it gladly. For Him it was like a badge of honor. But there were no women among "the twelve." That was only right. In our day women didn't travel with men who were not family. Scandal was always swirling around Jesus; He didn't want or need to fight that battle.

I've outlived all the rest of "the twelve" and His other followers. I can't tell you how lonely it is to be the last person with a memory, some would even say a fuzzy memory, of what Jesus looked like, the sound of His voice, the manner of His walk, the penetrating look in His eyes. All I can do is tell my story.

The Scripture says God knows the length of our days. Jesus reminded us that the Eternal has the hairs of our head numbered and knows when a little bird drops from the sky. So He knows how this feeble body aches. The mornings are the worst times.

I used to sleep—one of the benefits of a clean conscience, I suppose. But I don't sleep much anymore. Now these memories fill my thoughts. I constantly think about all those experiences of being with Jesus each day. So at night I think, I remember, I pray, I wait. I still look for His coming.

Some brothers have criticized me for my hope in His coming. They say that this is all that there is. What we have, of course, is great—the Spirit is strong with us, we have a vibrant community, God does things among us no one can explain—but still, I know there is more. I've seen it in His eyes. Oh, there's so much more.

So I wait.

Others criticize me for neglecting the blessed hope of His coming. I can't win. Because I speak so passionately of God's blessings now and how the Kingdom is with us now, some accuse me of forgetting about His coming. Nothing could be further from the truth.

Those of us who walked with Jesus were like most Jews in my village. We expected the Messiah to field an army, face off with the Romans, and reestablish the glory days of David and Solomon. We were completely disarmed by the simplicity and power of Jesus' voice, of His message. Only after the resurrection did the full weight settle in of what He said.

Before Jesus came along, many thought John the Immerser might be the Messiah. But when Jesus appeared in the wilderness, John pointed us to Him. The Immerser knew his place in God's redemptive plan. But there are still those who think he was more significant than Jesus. That movement is especially vocal in Ephesus. I feel like it is important for me to set the record straight. John the Immerser was a man sent from God. But Jesus is the Voice of God. John rejected any messianic claim outright. Jesus, though, accepted it with a smile, but only from a few of us—at least at first. Don't get me wrong, John was important, but he wasn't the Messiah. He preached repentance. He told us we were flawed—seriously flawed and we needed God's help. So he told everybody to get ready for One greater to come along. The One who comes will immerse us in fire and power, he said. John even told some of his followers to leave him and go follow Jesus.

Others have written accounts of what happened among us. I'd like to hear what they all have had to say. The ones I have heard have done a good job. But I have stories to tell no one is talking about. The other Gospels have faithfully portrayed the public Jesus. But I feel compelled to tell the story of the private Jesus. The others show us how Jesus preached and dealt with the multitudes. But I still remember the small group time with Jesus and the conversations that Jesus had with Nicodemus, the Samaritan woman, and the man born blind—I don't remember his name.

The other Gospels tell the tragedy and injustice of Jesus' death. Here was the single greatest man in history who was falsely accused; who was dragged before corrupt priests and a cruel Roman governor. He was condemned to death and crucified in a most hideous manner. On a human level, Jesus' arrest, condemnation, and crucifixion was a tragedy of epic proportions. But the more this old man thinks about what happened, the more I understand now that Jesus' death was His greatest hour. Things seemed to spin out of control so quickly. One minute we were celebrating the Passover together in the upper room; the next we were running for our lives! I'm not sure who was to blame for what happened to Jesus. Envious priests. The Roman governor. But, in fact, He was in complete control. That's why I say the hour of His death was the hour of His greatest glory. That's why I think that when Jesus was lifted up on the cross, He became the means by which all people can come to God. The most vivid memory that lingers in this old man's mind is of Jesus up there, on the cross. I can still see it like it was yesterday. His body—hanging halfway between heaven and earth, embracing the world—bridged the gap between God and humanity.

But I am getting way ahead of myself. There is one part of this fascinating story that I want to tell you about right now. Of all the things this old man has seen in his many years, the things that we saw and heard that week were the most startling.

Now I want to be very clear. This is my story, but unlike what you hear from most storytellers, this is completely true. I am giving you the testimony of an eyewitness. And like my brother disciples, I will swear upon my life that it is true.

John 13

¹Before the Passover festival began, Jesus was keenly aware that His hour had come to depart from this world and to return to the Father. From beginning to end, Jesus' days were marked by His love for His people. ²Before Jesus and His disciples gathered for dinner, the adversary filled Judas Iscariot's heart with plans of deceit and betrayal. ³Jesus, knowing that He had come from God and was going away to God, ⁴stood up from dinner and removed His outer garments. He then wrapped Himself in a towel, ⁵poured water in a basin, and began to wash the feet of the disciples, drying them with His towel.

Simon Peter	6	*(as Jesus approaches)* Lord, are You going to wash my feet?
Jesus	7	Peter, you don't realize what I am doing, but you will understand later.
Peter	8	You will not wash my feet, now or ever!

I have to interrupt the story so you can get the whole picture. Can you imagine what it would feel like to have Jesus (the creative force behind the entire cosmos) wash your feet?

Have you ever been in a gathering where a rich and powerful person offers to fill your glass? You are thinking, "I should do this myself. How is it that someone of your stature would be willing to serve me?" But later you find yourself serving those who would view you as rich and powerful in the same ways that you were

Jesus Washing the Disciples' Feet

served. Multiply that experience by thousands, and you will have a small glimpse of this powerful expression.

My life changed that day; there was a new clarity about how I was supposed to live. I saw the world in a totally new way. The dirt, grime, sin, pain, rebellion, and torment around me were no longer an impediment to the spiritual path—it was the path.

Where I saw pain and filth, I found an opportunity to extend God's kingdom through an expression of love, humility, and service. This simple act is a metaphor for the lens that Christ gives us to see the cosmos. He sees the people, the world He created—which He loves—He sees the filth, the corruption in the world that torments us. His mission is to cleanse those whom He loves from the horrors that torment them. This is His redemptive work with feet, families, disease, famine, and our hearts.

So many of you have missed the heart of the gospel and Christ's example. When you see sin exposed in people, you shake your head and think how sad it is. Or worse you look down at these people for their rejection of God, lack of understanding, and poor morals. This is not the way of Christ. When Christ saw disease, He saw the opportunity to heal. Where He saw sin, He saw a chance to forgive and redeem. When He saw dirty feet, He saw a chance to wash them.

What do you see when you wander through the market, along the streets, on the beaches, and through the slums? Are you disgusted? Or do you seize the opportunity to expand God's reign of love in the cosmos? This is what Jesus did. The places we avoid, Jesus seeks. Now I must digress to tell a bit of the story from long before. I remember Him leading our little group of disciples into one of the most wretched places I have ever seen. It was a series of pools where the crippled and diseased would gather in hopes of being healed. The stench was unbearable, and no sane person would march into an area littered with wretched bodies and communicable diseases. We followed Him reluctantly as He approached a crippled man on his mat and said to him, "Are you here in this place hoping to be healed?" The disabled man responded, "Kind Sir, I wait, like all of these people for the waters to stir, but I cannot walk. If I am to be healed by the waters, someone must carry me into the pool. So, the answer to Your question is yes—but I cannot be healed here unless someone will help me. Without a helping hand, someone else beats me to the water each time it is stirred." So, Jesus said, "Stand up, carry your mat and walk." At the moment Jesus uttered these words a healing energy coursed through the man and returned life to his limbs—he stood and walked for the first time in thirty-eight years (5:6-9).

It was not clear to us whether or not this man deserved this miracle. In fact, many of the disciples were disgusted by his lack of gratefulness and that he implicated Jesus to some of the Jewish authorities for healing him on the Sabbath. But God's grace is not earned; it is a beautiful gift to all of us.

When Jesus washed our feet He made an announcement to all who follow His path that life would not be about comfort, health, prosperity, and selfish pursuit.

I have gotten away from the story that was barely started. Let me back up and start almost from the beginning of the story again.

John 13

Simon Peter	6	*(as Jesus approaches)* Lord, are You going to wash my feet?
Jesus	7	Peter, you don't realize what I am doing, but you will understand later.
Peter	8	You will not wash my feet, now or ever!

Jesus		If I don't wash you, you will have nothing to do with Me.
Peter	**9**	Then wash me but don't stop with my feet. Cleanse my hands and head as well.
Jesus	**10**	Listen, anyone who has bathed is clean all over except for the feet. But I tell you this, not all of you are clean.

[11]He knew the one with plans of betraying Him, which is why He said, "not all of you are clean." [12]After washing their feet and picking up His garments, He reclined at the table again.

Jesus		Do you understand what I have done to you?
	13	You call Me Teacher and Lord, and truly, that is
	14	who I am. So, if your Lord and Teacher washes your feet, then you should wash one another's
	15	feet. I am your example; keep doing what I do.
	16	I tell you the truth: an apostle is not greater than the master. Those who are sent are not greater
	17	than the One who sends them. If you know these things, and if you put them into practice,
	18	you will find happiness. I am not speaking about all of you. I know whom I have chosen, but let the Scripture be fulfilled that says, "The very same man who eats My bread with Me, will
	19	stab Me in the back." Assuredly, I tell you these truths before they happen, so that when it all
	20	transpires you will believe that I am. I tell you the truth: anyone who accepts the ones I send accepts Me. In turn, the ones who accept Me, also accept the One who sent Me.

²¹Jesus was becoming visibly distressed.

| Jesus | I tell you the truth: one of you will betray Me. |

²²The disciples began to stare at one another, wondering who was the unfaithful disciple. ²³One disciple in particular, who was loved by Jesus, reclined next to Him at the table. ²⁴Peter motioned to the disciple at Jesus' side.

Peter		(to the beloved disciple) Find out who the betrayer is.
Beloved Disciple	25	(leaning in to Jesus) Lord, who is it?
Jesus	26	I will dip a piece of bread in My cup and give it to the one who will betray Me.

He dipped one piece in the cup and gave it to Judas, the son of Simon Iscariot. ²⁷After this occurred, Satan entered into Judas.

| Jesus | (to Judas) Make haste, and do what you are going to do. |

²⁸No one understood Jesus' instructions to Judas. ²⁹Because Judas carried the money, some thought he was being instructed to buy the necessary items for the feast, or give some money to the poor. ³⁰So Judas took his piece of bread and departed into the night.
³¹Upon Judas' departure, Jesus spoke:

| Jesus | 32 | Now the Son of Man will be glorified as God is glorified in Him. If God's glory is in Him, His glo is also in God. The moment of this astounding |

	33	glory is imminent. My children, My time here is brief. You will be searching for Me, and as I told the Jews, "You cannot go where I am going."
	34	So, I give you a new command: Love each other deeply and fully. Remember the ways that I have loved you, and demonstrate your love for
	35	others in those same ways. Everyone will know you as followers of Christ if you demonstrate your love to others.
Simon Peter	36	Lord, where are You going?
Jesus		Peter, you cannot come with Me now, but later you will join Me.
Peter	37	Why can't I go now? I'll give my life for You!
Jesus	38	Will you really give your life for Me? I tell you the truth: you will deny Me three times before the rooster crows.

Ultimately, Peter was telling the truth. He was more than willing to lay down his life. But none of us understood the magnitude of the persecution and hatred that was about to be unleashed on all of us. You ask me, "Did that change the way you led and treated people in your community or outside of it? Some of us think you have an ax to grind with the Jews. What connection did this pattern of living have with Jesus' command to love? How can you reconcile your angst against the Jews and this command Christ gave you to love?"